After finishing university, you should be smart enough to spot a good deal when you see one.

As a graduate, we can offer you a first class package including:

● Special offers on graduate overdrafts and loans.

● Primeline, our 24 hour person-to-person telephone banking service.

● Commission-free travellers cheques and currency.

● And many other benefits.

If you'd like more details, simply call us on the number below.

0800 200 400
Monday-Friday 8am-8pm, Saturday 9am-6pm
www.natwest.co.uk

NatWest
More than just a bank

Credit is only available to persons over the age of majority and is subject to terms and conditions. Written quotations are available on request from National Westminster Bank Plc 41 Lothbury, London EC2P 2BP. Registered number 929027 England. We may monitor and record your phone calls with us in order to maintain and improve our service. Ref. No. TG98

IT could help your career.

The revolution in Information Technology is affecting most of us and will continue to do so. Even if you do not plan to specialise in computers, you will probably need to use them. Almost every occupation – from administration to zoology – uses this all-embracing technology. For example, it helps in communicating with other people; in planning and managing work; in producing documents; and in research, design and development.

Information Technology, sometimes called "IT", offers a wealth of career opportunities. Whether you are more interested in the products or working with people, you can select from a wide range of occupations to suit your interests and career plans.

Even if your sights are set on a different profession, IT is still relevant. To increase your potential you need to take charge of your own career plans, and to consider your development needs. Have you developed to your own satisfaction those core skills needed for most occupations? Those skills are in working with others, numerical ability, communication, and IT.

Maybe you are already well established in a career. IT competence can help you become even more effective in your chosen profession. It can become an important tool in your portfolio of skills.

Or maybe you want to spread your wings and become self-employed. Here a mastery of the personal computer can help you set up your own office quickly, and achieve that desired independence.

If you have family commitments which require you to be at home, a mastery of IT can give you the freedom to take on work which otherwise might not have been available.

The IT National Training Organisation (IT NTO) provides a framework for the development of all skills in IT. We have successful IT Modern Apprenticeship and National Traineeship programmes to support IT-dependent occupations. We work in partnership with other organisations involved in education, training, and professional development: such as the British Computer Society, training providers, Government Departments (DTI and DfEE), and the Training and Enterprise councils.

To find out more about how we can help you, please telephone 0171 580 6677, send us a fax on 0171 580 5577, or email to info@itnto.org.uk.

It could help your career.

iv

Leicester
COLLEGE

Library books are to be returned on or before the last date below.
Tel. Freemen's Park 0116 2242046
Bede Island 0116 2242111
St Margaret's 0116 2242160
Abbey Park 0116 2244100

Developing
Your
Employment
Skills

Bought from
Leicester College
26-10-2010

50p

TROTMAN

This first edition published in 1998 by Trotman and Company Ltd
12 Hill Rise, Richmond, Surrey TW10 6UA

© Trotman and Company Limited 1998

British Library Cataloguing in Publication Data
A catalogue record for this book is available from the British Library

ISBN 0 85660 308 2

Typeset by Trotman and Company, Richmond
Printed and bound in Great Britain by Creative Print & Design (Wales) Ltd

Contents

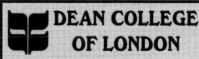

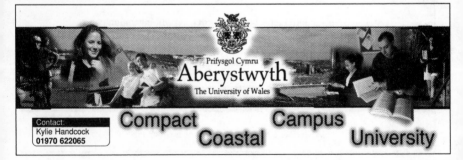

Introduction

The concept of a career is altering with the changing world of business and industry. There is no longer a 'job for life', with all the trappings of long-term security that it implies. There's less structure to career progression or automatic rise in income as the years move on. It's going to be much more of a struggle to find the opportunities – and secure them – as our working lives progress. Jobs are more likely to be stepping stones to a goal rather than the goal itself.

New skills

These new conditions require a different set of skills. Negotiating, networking, planning and presentation are going to be fundamental to an individual's success. These might be assets we've taken for granted before, believing that all we need in our jobs are academic qualifications and signs of competence. They are no longer enough. We're all going to have to focus much more on identifying and developing the specific aptitudes we need to maintain our employability.

People's perception of work is changing. It is no longer something done purely for money, but increasingly being seen as a way of finding a new and stimulating direction which will lead to personal fulfilment. As these changes gather pace, so attitudes towards work are altering fast. Already people are adjusting their approach, beginning to welcome diversity and set it within the desire for a balanced lifestyle.

People expect a job to offer a challenge and an opportunity for self-development. It's not only good money that motivates people to work now. Other elements such as variety and interest in a job are just as important – if not more so.

The impact of technology

As people have to – or choose to – change from one job to another and into new areas of work, they need to add to their education and possibly undergo training. Technological change is having a huge impact on the nature and structure of organisations. No one wants yesterday's product – the pace of development has to keep up with – or ahead of – the demands of an ever-hungry consumer market. If you are involved in design, manufacture, marketing and advertising consumer goods, you have to make sure that your knowledge and expertise is kept constantly up to scratch.

Changing ways of working

Ways of working are changing just as quickly. Organisations are 'flattening' their structures, removing whole layers of hierarchy, and almost everyone is affected. Working practices have to be modified to deal with new pressures and requirements. As a result, more and more people have to face up to the stark reality that their education, which they thought they had finished with years ago, no longer gives them the competence they need. Sometimes they are even finding that the very job they trained for is itself becoming extinct. And the onus is on them to make sure they have the skills they're going to need for the next role in their working life.

Education, learning and careers guidance have traditionally been seen as processes that begin and end with school or college. Once we leave adolescence, we are deemed to have completed all the development we need and can move on to a comparatively change-free adulthood.

Well it's different now; outlooks are changing. People are taking on the trappings of adulthood later and later, delaying the responsibilities which are normally attached to maturity – a family, a steady job, and so forth. And, as change is thrust upon them, so is the need to continue with education and learning, accessing careers advice and guidance at various stages. Around half of all the students at universities around the UK are mature students – that is, aged over 25. People are having to take responsibility for their own learning and personal development.

We are all going to need to be much more adaptable, to allow (and even encourage) our careers to evolve – and we're going to have to develop the flexibility and confidence to cope with uncertainty and change.

About this book

This book is a guide to developing the skills you need to maintain your employability. It will tell you:

- what skills are and why we need them
- how to identify the skills you have – and those you lack
- how to develop the skills you need
- other strategies that could help pinpoint your goals
- where to find out more.

CHAPTER 1

Why do we need skills?

Skills lie at the very heart of our success – not just for each of us personally, but for businesses, and ultimately for the prosperity of the whole country. In an increasingly competitive and fast-moving world, employers want people who have a wide range of skills to bring to the work environment.

In the past the majority of people tended to concentrate on one area of work throughout their working lives. They would be a motor mechanic or a medic, a secretary or a solicitor. Once they had landed a job, and perhaps risen up the career ladder, that was it – they had it made! They could be virtually sure of a secure future – and a meal ticket for life. Nowadays things have changed.

Because of the effects of world recession, the efficiency of information technology and telecommunications and the impact of leaner businesses (involving 'downsizing' or 'rightsizing', 'delayering' and 'outsourcing'), there is more need for a flexible, adaptable workforce which is 'multiskilled' and can fulfil many different roles. Employers have to be sure that the people who work for them do the tasks necessary for the business to run smoothly and effectively – and keep up with (or ahead of) the competition.

And if you want to improve – or even maintain – your employability, the best way to do that is to train and develop your skills. In short, *stay marketable!*

Quicklist of terms

Downsizing – reducing the number of employees

Rightsizing – making a company a viable size

Delayering – getting rid of 'vertical' (hierarchical) management structures

Outsourcing – putting elements of a job out to contract

Branching out

Whereas people used to stick to their own job function, carrying out part of a wider process, today they tend to work in teams, sharing a whole range of tasks. If you work on a production line, for instance, you are now likely to be familiar with all aspects of that line and be able to turn your hand to any part of it at any time. It makes your job more interesting – and it's more useful to your employer because it makes the staffing possibilities more flexible.

If yours is a professional role, projects originally worked on in isolation are now likely to be tackled in a multidisciplinary team, involving a range of professionals from different specialisms, building on progress together. In the NHS, for instance, community teams comprising health visitors, district nurses, physiotherapists, occupational therapists and social workers, work together to provide care for the whole community. It's a way of producing a more efficient service – within a more streamlined structure.

In addition, more responsibility is being passed further down organisations. And that leads not only to a greater demand for a wider range of better developed skills, it also results in more satisfying jobs for many more people.

The down side is the effect that all this reorganisation has had on staffing numbers. Unemployment has risen. And those employees enjoying the jobs which remain are likely to have greater levels of responsibility – and stress – along with their job fulfilment. All the more reason, then, to be sure that you are constantly developing the skills you need to keep on top.

Filling the gaps

You may feel that flexibility doesn't apply to your job – you are fine doing what's requested of you and there's no need to expand that. Or your role only requires you to do a limited range of tasks – anything extra would be unnecessary. But now that a job for life is a thing of the past, it is the people who have developed a range of skills who will succeed in their changing careers, and be sought after by employers.

If you can identify gaps in your skills knowledge – and fill those gaps – you will be of more use to your employer, you'll enhance your career prospects and you'll find life more rewarding.

Filling those skills gaps can give you:
- ▌ better career opportunities with your present employer
- ▌ new opportunities for different jobs
- ▌ increased self-motivation and self-fulfilment.

Take a look at the list below and tick those that apply to you.

❑	My role is neatly defined – and I'm happy with that.
❑	My role is defined – but I wish it weren't.
❑	I have to do a variety of tasks.
❑	I have skills which I don't use – but could if asked.
❑	There are plenty of things I'd like to do – but I don't know how.

If you are happy as you are, that's fine – as long as you are not left behind. If you are currently too restricted or you feel you could do more, you hope to take a new direction or find a job you *really* want, there are plenty of things you can do to make progress. You could:
- ▌ train for other job functions
- ▌ take a course to extend your knowledge
- ▌ learn a new skill, such as word-processing or a language
- ▌ broaden your own interests
- ▌ talk about how you can use your skills in your everyday life.

There are opportunities for you to develop your skills in all areas and at every level, depending on your needs and interests. You can read how throughout this book. Every addition you make will help to build a fuller and more comprehensive 'portfolio' to offer to an employer. In short, a more marketable you.

We're talking here not just about skills which you can demonstrate through your academic qualifications – a degree in marketing or engineering, for instance, a diploma in hotel management or a certificate in keyboard skills. These all show valuable skills, of course. But there are more.

There are those less definable 'personal transferable' skills which are vital if the business of day-to-day work is going to be successful – such as communication skills, problem-solving or team-working. You can read more about skills and what they are in Chapter 2.

Providing employment skills

These broader skills all help to make you more effective in your present job, and more likely to have that added bonus of job satisfaction. But they are just as important when it comes to helping you develop the kind of 'profile' an employer wants.

Having these skills gives you something extra to offer – and something which will be invaluable in a work situation, where you are dealing with other people. It means that an employer can be fairly sure that you can contribute something positive to the overall success of the business, over and above the skills which allow you simply to do your job. And that applies whether you are in work at the moment or hoping to move to something new.

You'll see in Chapter 6 how you can read between the lines to work out what an employer is looking for, and how you can then match that skills profile. Developing their skills is something that plenty of people have done before, and that more and more people are beginning to do as they hear about the benefits.

Sally is a packer in a food processing company. She was persuaded by her manager to take a Business Studies course and a Basic Maths course and she hasn't looked back since. 'After the Business Studies course I began to look at my own job differently to see if there were ways in which I could improve it. It makes you start spotting mistakes and sorting them out. And the Maths course has helped me a lot too. I'd been a bit worried about studying again but I feel much more self-assured since I took my courses – so much so that I went on to do a language course. Languages are useful in the factory – when we have foreign visitors we can actually talk to them about what we're doing rather than just dumbly standing there!'

An important factor for Sally has been her family's response. 'I've only ever been a wife and mum. It amazed my family that I would actually sit down and do a Business course. They look at me in a new light now. And I look at myself and say, "You have passed these exams – at your age!" And I'm quite impressed. It's given me a lot more confidence.'

Alan is a fitter who is looking to move to a different section.

'I know I'm not going to be doing the same job in the future, so I've decided to get myself equipped and learn new skills. I've enrolled on a welding course. It's a case of helping myself as well as the company. There are things which you can do for yourself and this is one of them. In the past people left school, got a job and didn't think much about training. You can't do that now. You just have to develop for the sake of your job – and your future.

'Because of the welding course I'm finding that I'm having a go at jobs at work that I probably wouldn't have had a go at before. And I know that if the worse came to the worst I could sell myself more easily on the job market than I could have done before because I've got more strings to my bow.'

Lifelong learning

However good your general education and initial training for work, it's more important than ever before to keep up to date so that you don't get left behind. The constant innovation in technology and the rapid pace of change within organisations means that we all have to continue learning throughout our working lives (and why stop there?)

We all need to learn in order to be adaptable at work. But the idea of lifelong learning isn't solely to add to our capabilities at work. It also plays a key role in our life away from work – in our social activities with friends, in our appreciation of culture and leisure pursuits. Like ripples in a pond, learning for work can reverberate through all aspects of our lives – a course which relates directly to work can not only enhance your job, it can also make you a more interesting person outside work. In the same way, a course of study which has nothing whatsoever to do with work (such as flower arranging or golf lessons) can give you so much satisfaction that you have more to give back in the workplace.

Taking a course of study can:

▌ increase your confidence
▌ make you more assertive
▌ help you widen your circle of friends

- broaden your horizons
- make you more interesting.

It really can enrich your life!

Using skills development to change direction

Developing skills doesn't just help in your current job, or the career area you had assumed was right for you. As you'll see in Chapter 4, you can use them to take you exactly where you want to go.

Matthew is a computer specialist working for a large organisation in the Midlands, but he's developing his skills to change career completely. Still keeping his daytime job, he registered with the Chartered Association of Certified Accountants (ACCA), going along to his local university two evenings a week.

'I first became interested in accountancy through talking to accountant friends, but in the last few years I've become increasingly keen on money management and business. I like to keep up to date with the financial pages and decided some time ago that I wanted a career in finance. I did a Basic Bookkeeping course a while ago and enjoyed that, so this seemed the obvious next step in my development. It will take me at least three or four years to complete the theoretical side, and then I'll need an extra three years' relevant practical experience to gain the qualification, but it will all be worth it in the end.

'I've already let my employers know that I would really like to transfer to the finance section. It seemed the ideal thing to do to take this ACCA course while I'm waiting for an opening, in the hope that my qualifications will stand me in good stead. It's tough, mostly because of the sheer volume of work involved, but it's been good discipline for me and a way of using my brain.'

In brief

Skills development can:
- make you and the company you work for more effective
- make you more employable
- broaden your outlook
- enrich your experience
- open up doors.

CHAPTER 2

What are skills?

'Skills' mean different things to different people. Clearly, if you are going to develop employment skills, you need to identify first what they are. Skills can be divided broadly into:

▮ basic skills
▮ transferable skills
▮ employment skills.

And they are all important in their different ways.

BASIC SKILLS ensure that you can 'hold your own' in your community on a day-to-day basis – reading, writing and using basic arithmetic. TRANSFERABLE skills are the 'jam on the bread' – skills which you can use in all kinds of environments. EMPLOYMENT skills are made up of a range of talents and abilities from both the skills groups.

Basic skills

Basic skills are literacy and numeracy. Literacy is the ability to read, write and speak English. Numeracy is being able to use maths at a level that will let you get by in work and general living.

These are the essential skills that everyone needs to function effectively in today's society. If you haven't got a good grasp of basic skills, you are at a serious disadvantage when it comes to competition for jobs. You also face a sizeable barrier when it comes to taking further learning to improve your skills base.

Once you have improved these, you can move on to the transferable skills that will bring you higher economic and social returns.

Theresa is a packer at a bakery in the Midlands. She'd always had problems with maths so decided to join a class run at work. She was worried about taking the Basic Maths course, but her mind was soon put at rest.

'The tutor was really patient and understanding. She sat me down and told me not to panic. I appreciated that. I didn't know what I was getting into because when I was at school it wasn't like it is now. Going in for this course has enlightened me a lot though. There's a lot of new technology in our factory. Doing this course has given me confidence in myself and my job. I found it a lot of fun.'

Transferable skills

Transferable skills are the ones you can take with you from one job to another and use in any role in life. They build upon the basic skills, but they are broader in their scope. Also known as 'core skills', they are thought of as particularly necessary for employability – whatever your job and at whatever level.

Transferable skills include those which can be measured – such as information technology or language skills – as well as less tangible attributes such as self-motivation and initiative.

They are the sort of skills that don't stand still. They need to be nurtured and nourished so that they are kept fresh and vital. They are the ones we will all need more and more into the 21st century. They are skills which enable us to be self-reliant and to cope effectively in a changing world. The following are just some transferable skills. As you will see, many of them are interrelated:

- self-awareness
- self-management
- interpersonal skills
- flexibility
- communication
- problem solving
- team-working
- business awareness
- networking
- negotiation

- leadership
- computer literacy
- language skills
- driving ability

If you concentrate on developing these skills, you will be a well-rounded, self-reliant and confident individual – and there will be no reason why you shouldn't be right at the very front of the queue when it comes to personal career growth.

But what does each of these skills really mean?

Self-awareness

Self-awareness is crucial if you are going to succeed in a competitive world. It means that you know yourself – your capabilities and your limitations. You know where you are and where you want to go.

If you are self-aware, you can:
- identify your skills
- analyse what makes you tick and what you feel is important
- learn from past experiences
- pinpoint your strengths and what makes you stand out from other people (your added value)
- record and assess these attributes
- take – and give – constructive criticism
- recognise the areas where you need to develop.

CASE study

Sarah gave up her job as a secretary when she got married and had children. Twenty years later she looked at her skills levels and was totally honest with herself.

'I realised that technology had moved on dramatically since I was last in an office. I knew I had certain strengths which won't date (such as being well organised and working well with other people), but I knew no one would employ me now unless I updated my skills. I found out about the NVQ level 4 in Business Administration which was just what I was looking for. It builds on my previous skills and knowledge so that ultimately I will have more to offer an employer.'

Sarah's course is for one year full time, with one day a week on work experience.

What are skills? **21**

'It's been a huge success. Around half the students are over 30, so I feel comfortable. And the tutors consciously take a more flexible approach to accommodate the outside commitments of mature students. I'm now waiting to hear about a jobsharing role which itself would lead to more training and personal development. It could open up a promising career.'

Self-management

Self-management means that you can work alone or almost alone, without the need for someone to stand over you constantly and tell you what to do. If you are a good self-manager, you can:

- organise your life – both in and out of work
- work unsupervised
- motivate yourself to complete tasks
- manage your time effectively, balancing working hard with being sociable!
- prioritise, sorting out what's important and what's not
- know when to say no – and be able to do so.
- plan your next steps – and see them through.

Graham lost his job, his business and his home during the recession. He applied for jobs but fierce competition convinced him that he needed to plan where he wanted to go, find out what he needed to do to get there – then set his mind to it.

'I'd always wanted to study but I left school at 15 and never had the opportunity. I soon found myself with a family to support and things just developed from there. But when my life fell apart I had no other option – I had to take stock. It was difficult studying with five children around me, living in just two rooms. But once I'd organised myself and my time I just got my head down. I've mapped out where I want to go and I'm determined to get there. This whole experience has given me the self-discipline – and now the skills – to press on with my plans.'

Graham has now studied his way to completing a part-time Honours degree in Business.

'However bad things get I always have a positive outlook. I now know I can achieve anything I set my mind to. All it takes is good organisation and determination. Learning has given me a ladder out of the abyss.'

Interpersonal skills

Interpersonal skills are at the centre of your success. If you are going to get on at all, you need to be able to relate well to other people. If you have effective interpersonal skills, you can:

- judge what behaviour is appropriate, and when to use it (such as not criticising someone in public – or making a pass at the boss's husband)
- put people at their ease
- make people feel valued
- be relaxed with all kinds of people
- encourage people to contribute their ideas
- put across a negative message in a tactful way
- be interested and interesting.

Ruth is a nurse in a busy children's ward, where her people skills are vital day in, day out.

'I'm dealing with people all the time – children, their parents, doctors and other professional staff. Parents are likely to be anxious or worried, the children can be frightened or in pain. I need to be able to judge situations and make everyone feel as comfortable as possible. It makes an enormous difference to the quality of their care.'

Flexibility

Flexibility is vital in a world where no role at work is guaranteed. It means that you have an open mind which will spot opportunities as they arise – and create new ones. If you are flexible, you can:

- assess different situations and act appropriately
- turn your hand to anything that's needed
- adapt to changing circumstances
- see new ways of approaching problems
- work with all kinds of people
- understand what's necessary
- undertake new ways of working.

*Melissa says that she wasn't much good at maths at school –
yet here she is as a currency dealer in Europe.*

'I've really adapted to changing circumstances as I went along. I began with a psychology degree at university, then when I heard of an opportunity to teach abroad I took a Teaching English as a Foreign Language (TEFL) quali-fication. That job unfortunately fell through but, undeterred, I began to look around for other options. A friend was a banker in Luxembourg and he told me that there were lots of openings there with banks. I weighed up all the pros and cons – and bought my plane ticket. I figured the worst that could happen would be that I'd have a good holiday – at best I'd have a new career! I took a job as a waitress while I scanned the job ads and finally applied to be a trainee dealer on the money markets. I'd got no experience, but the main qualification needed was character – and I'm certainly adapt-able and determined! Two years later, I haven't looked back.'

Communication

It goes without saying that if we want to get a message across, we need good communication skills.

Communication is our basic means of making ourselves heard. It's the only way we have of letting other people know both good and bad news – and of blowing our own trumpet!

If you have good communication skills, you can:

■ write and speak effectively – in written reports, over the telephone and in visual presentations
■ convey the message you are trying to relate
■ appreciate other people's moods and needs
■ adopt the appropriate tone
■ be sure that people will listen to you
■ work well in teams, with others
■ listen as well as broadcast!

study

*William is a graphic designer, who's learned a thing or two
about communication skills.*

'I found out very quickly that in this business if you want to get on you have got to be able to communicate well. Clients have to feel sure that they've given the right person the contract, so you have to be able to communicate your ideas with confidence, explaining clearly so that they understand what you are aiming for. It means that they're much more likely to be delighted with the job when it's finished, and that you are more likely to get repeat work the next time.'

Problem solving

The ability to solve problems is required of more people than ever, as responsibility cascades down through organisations as they become flatter structures. If you are good at problem solving, you can:

■ collect and collate information
■ analyse different situations
■ appreciate all sides of a problem
■ think laterally
■ anticipate the consequences of your actions
■ reach solutions that work
■ be creative – but realistic – in your suggestions.

What does an Outward Bound course have to do with problem solving – and how could it possibly change your attitude to your job? That's exactly what Robert thought. He's a forklift truck driver for a firm in Devon, and the great outdoors had always been far from his mind until he was persuaded to take part in a weekend course.

'I'd never done anything like it before. We went abseiling, kayaking, mountain climbing, and on an assault course. At various points we were set problems which we had to solve – like building a bridge to cross a gully, which we all had to use. It kept you thinking all the time, exercising the brain as well as the body. By the end I'd realised I can get my head round problems if I try – and I got a great sense of achievement out of it. Now if I come across hitches at work, I can solve the problem myself, with confidence.'

Team-working

Team-working is becoming important for more and more people as different ways of working are established. Working as part of a team could involve working with others in a similar function – such as machining dressmaking pieces in a clothing factory, or collaborating with people from different professional disciplines to produce an overall picture of a set of circumstances – such as a surveyor, a planner, a builder, an architect and an engineer all working together to produce a finished building.

If you team-work, you need to be able to:

- build a good relationship with other people
- be able to communicate well with the rest of your team
- work at maintaining good relationships
- be able to take a back seat when necessary
- build on other people's ideas
- make useful contributions
- persuade people to your own point of view.

Sometimes the least likely pursuits can develop useful skills. You just need to think laterally, as they found at a clothing factory in Yorkshire.

'We've all decided to take over the top floor of the local Superbowl to have an inter-company Ten Pin Bowling Challenge. The rivalry has been fierce from the start. We've got 12 teams altogether, with families and friends as supporters to cheer them along. Everyone gets free bowling and a meal. The idea is to really stir up interest and motivation in developing skills – after all, bowling is team-building! It's useful, stimulating – and fun! We've improved interpersonal and communication skills as people have found a common goal. And these transfer easily to the workplace.'

Business awareness

Business awareness is a skill that is increasingly in demand in every area of work. It means that you understand what drives a business and how it works. If you have good business awareness, you can:

- understand that a business needs to make profits
- identify activities which are cost effective
- avoid ideas which will spell financial disaster, however appealing they may sound
- appreciate the need for development
- see possibilities for change
- understand the hidden tensions and power struggles that exist in any organisation
- identify the source of the power behind the business.

Paul has his own news agents in a village in Cumbria. He wanted his staff to realise that, even though the work seems much the same, year in, year out, the business had to develop all the time – and that their involvement in that would make all the difference – to them all.

'I heard about NVQs and found out that they could really benefit us all. I took a qualification which enables me to assess staff at work and now they're all working towards qualifications which recognise what they do, and give them more insight into the business. They're always coming up with new ideas and consequently I have more valuable staff – and they have a more interesting life.'

Networking

Networking is a skill that will stand you in good stead both in and out of work. It is a way of building up a range of contacts for advice and information, and every strand of the web can benefit from another. Networking involves:

■ working out where you need to make contacts – and why
■ identifying the right person to link with
■ making contact (by phone, in writing or in person)
■ building the link
■ maintaining the relationship
■ keeping good records of the network so you know where to look next time
■ *using* the network once you have built it.

Charlotte is an interior designer whose business depends on building up a clientele – and making sure they come back for more.

'I started my business from scratch, so it was a question of networking like mad to get my name known. I had business cards printed and made sure that they got to all the right people. I went to trade fairs and exhibitions and made myself go and talk to people I thought might be able to help. In the end it paid off – I was offered a magazine column and have just been approached to see if I'd like to branch into television.'

Negotiation

Negotiation is all about getting what you want – nicely! If you have good negotiation skills, you can:

- identify your goals before you begin
- map out a plan of action
- communicate effectively
- be assertive without being aggressive
- be willing to compromise when necessary
- know when to press your case, and when to give in gracefully
- make everyone feel there are no losers – just winners (known as a 'win/win' agreement).

> *Tony wasn't happy with changes affecting working conditions, but he knew he had to tread carefully to reach a compromise.*

'Although we were all becoming more and more cross about the way we were being treated, I knew if we lost our tempers we'd get nowhere. In the end I made an appointment with the boss and we talked things through calmly. Between us we managed to find a way forward to suit us both. It was a question of being able to compromise and understand each other's viewpoint.'

Leadership

Leadership skills aren't just for those few at the very top of the tree – although of course they're vital if you happen to be in that position. Leadership skills are about steering an issue or a group of people, about taking decisions – and seeing them through, and sometimes they're about looking after the interests of people whose skills of self-reliance aren't so well developed.

Leadership skills mean you can:

- make decisions
- manage people to achieve a range of tasks
- encourage people to be well motivated in what they do
- take an interest in the people around you
- not crumble at times of crisis
- take responsibility on a day-to-day basis
- carry the can when things go wrong.

Suzanne is works manager at a plating company in Yorkshire. When she started the job, the staff were demoralised and the company was losing money. Her leadership helped turn the business round.

'I knew that to get things going again the staff needed to be working together and valuing themselves as a vital part of a team. I introduced team briefings for people to air any problems or queries, which I then sorted out. I helped them solve their problems at home so that they could be more effective at work. And I multiskilled them by giving them additional training so that they could feel confident doing any job. By showing that I'll work for them, they become more highly motivated and prepared to produce what I need in return. In this way we've built up a solid relationship and morale has increased tremendously.'

The next three are FUNCTIONAL skills. They can be transferred from one situation to another, but they are skills which involve competence at a particular function.

Computer literacy

It won't be long before computer literacy is required in almost every working role. Being computer literate means you can work various computer functions, eg word-processing, spreadsheets and databases.

Malcolm is an operator in a factory in Kent and was apprehensive about taking a computer course.

'I've never kept up with my kids when it comes to computers, so the whole idea was rather daunting. But we're going through so much change as a site and expectations of operators have changed – we may be expected to move plants and take different jobs – I realised that to get myself better trained would help me have a more stable future. I'd been nervous about "going back to school", but in the event it's been more like an evening out, not an ordeal. Not only have I found it stimulating, it's also given me skills which are really relevant nowadays.'

Language skills

It's true – the world is getting smaller! As companies do business in a wider and wider arc – not only in Europe but as far afield as South

America, Africa and the Pacific Rim, for example – there is going to be more emphasis on employing staff who can speak a language in addition to English.

A business which can communicate with all its customers in their own language is going to be a cut above the rest, and a person who offers language skills to a prospective employer will be a step ahead of the competition on a shortlist of applicants. Some of the most useful languages are French, German, Spanish, Russian, Japanese and any Eastern European language, not to mention Italian, Arabic or Urdu, depending on a company's area of specialism.

Many organisations nowadays deal with European businesses – buy European equipment, deal with European customers and even host European workers in the factory. But factory workers are often ill-equipped to deal with people who aren't fluent in English.

Sam is a factory worker at a car manufacturers, which found that when foreigners came no one could communicate with them. Everyone felt they were giving of poor impression of themselves and the company, so Sam and some colleagues decided to take an Italian language course.

'We can now offer our services to host foreign visitors, both around the factory and outside on a social basis. We can also act as interpreters when other departments are stuck. We believe now that we can harness all manner of skills on site. It's very exciting.'

Driving ability

A common transferable skill which most of us take for granted is the ability to drive – a car, a van, a lorry. It can be essential for some jobs that you are able to show a clean driving licence and, as appropriate, licences for: heavy good vehicles (HGVs); passenger carrying vehicles (PCVs); or volunteer driving (eg local authority) permits.

Jackie felt that her retail career could go no further, but simply learning to drive changed her prospects dramatically.

'I'd never got around to driving lessons, but when they offered me a job that would involve travelling to our different stores I knew that it could give me the opportunity I wanted. I took some lessons and even passed first time. Not only could I take the job I was offered, being able to drive has immense benefits in terms of my self-confidence. And my freedom!'

Employment skills

Employment skills combine basic and transferable skills, adding in the specific skills you need for a particular job. For example, if you want to become an accountant, you are going to need basic literacy and numeracy as well as some of the transferable skills, but you will also have to pass relevant professional exams which develop the particular skills you need for that job. Employment skills are those which you build up through studying and through experience in a job.

The majority of jobs nowadays require skills which are relevant to that area of work – skills which you can learn through a combination of further or higher education courses and work-based experience. Even those jobs which don't have such requirements now offer a route to getting work-based skills formally recognised, via training and certification. Certification confirming a skill level is a straight-forward way of transferring your skills from one job to another, and acts as a stepping-stone to improve your career prospects.

Laura had been working in the retail industry for several years but really wanted to go into publishing.
'I managed to get a place at university to read English, and followed that with a postgraduate course in journalism. All the while I was building up my experience through editing the university newspaper and helping out at the local trade paper. It all served to develop the skills I needed to get me where I wanted to be in the end – in the thick of things at a magazine.'

In brief

Skills can be divided into:
- basic – reading, writing and arithmetic
- transferable – skills which you can take with you from one job to another
- employment skills – a combination of the two.

PART2 YOURSKILLS
Getting started

How can you develop your skills? How do you even work out what skills you need? How do you know what skills you already have? How do you take the first step in acquiring new skills? If you have never thought about your skills levels before, this can sound rather daunting.

There are certain steps that everyone can take to improve their skills – and their employability. You need to:

- identify the skills you already have (and at what level)
- work out your skills gaps
- decide whether and how to fill them.

Identify the skills you have – and work out the gaps

Before you can identify the gaps, you need to work out what skills you already have. Some of these will be obvious for most people. For example, if your job is as a computer programmer, the chances are that you can tick off 'computer literacy' as one of your competencies right away. If you are an interpreter, languages are an obvious achievement. And if you are an HGV driver, driving ability is already yours.

Basic literacy and numeracy

Basic literacy and numeracy – ability with words and numbers – are also reasonably easy to define. Do you have difficulty reading, writing or speaking English? Can you add up well enough to cope in the shops and with day-to-day bills? If you need help in these areas, don't worry, there are steps you can take. Get in touch with your local **careers service** (see pages 30–32), **Jobcentre, Jobclub, drop-in centre** or **college** and ask for details of help available near you.

Transferable skills

Transferable skills are much harder to pinpoint, particularly when you are talking about yourself.

Most of us find it comparatively difficult to be totally objective about our own abilities. Talking to a friend, a colleague at work or a 'mentor' can help you analyse your strong points and identify your shortcomings.

> **A mentor:** someone who can help you work out what you have got, where you want to go, and what you need to get there. Read more about mentors on page 55.

Think about your **strengths** and **weaknesses**. What do you enjoy doing – and feel reasonably confident that you do well? What situations do you find yourself avoiding time and again?

Think first about your experiences at work. Then broaden out the picture to your life at home and in social situations. Jot down any examples that come to mind which demonstrate your effectiveness (or terror!) in a situation. For instance, are you the kind of person who always gets the best deal on the goods you buy or the holidays you take? Do you find yourself with the best seats in a restaurant (without resorting to bribes)? Do people always fall in with your suggestions (without your being bossy)?

If the answer to all these is 'yes', it could be because you can use the following skills effectively:

- negotiation
- interpersonal skills
- leadership.

The following prompts might help you relate your everyday life to your personal skills analysis.

SELF-AWARENESS

- Do you know what makes you tick?
- Can you describe your strengths and weaknesses?
- Can you cope with criticism?

SELF-MANAGEMENT

- Are you good at managing your time?

- Can you get things done without being pushed?
- Are you good at planning – and seeing plans through?

INTERPERSONAL SKILLS
- Are you good at judging just the right thing to say?
- Can you put people at ease quickly?
- Do you mix well with all kinds of people?

FLEXIBILITY
- Can you assess the demands of different circumstances?
- Do you adapt well to different situations?
- Do you see new ways of approaching problems?

COMMUNICATION
- Are you good at writing letters and reports?
- Are you sensitive to other people's moods?
- Are you a good listener as well as a good speaker?

PROBLEM SOLVING
- Can you collect and analyse information?
- Do you see all sides of a problem?
- Can you reach creative solutions – that work?

TEAM-WORKING
- Are you good at building – and maintaining – relationships with other people?
- Can you take a back seat when necessary?
- Can you build on ideas with other people?

BUSINESS AWARENESS
- Do you appreciate the need for business development?
- Can you identify ideas which are cost effective?
- Do you understand business 'politics'?

NETWORKING
- Can you identify people who might be useful to you?

- Are you good at making contact with them?
- Do you then keep up those links?

NEGOTIATION

- Do you know what you are aiming for when you start a discussion?
- Are you assertive without being aggressive?
- Can you give in gracefully?

LEADERSHIP

- Are you good at making decisions – and taking responsibility?
- Can you motivate people?
- Are you good in a crisis?

COMPUTER LITERACY

- Can you use a spreadsheet?
- Are you good at word-processing?
- What about databases?

LANGUAGE SKILLS

- Are you at least at GCSE level in another language?
- Can you use the business vocabulary of that language?
- Are you confident enough to speak to prospective clients?

DRIVING ABILITY

- Have you a current, clean driving licence?

Now you are ready to write your skills profile, which will allow you to assess your current skills levels. Start by writing down the skills you use everyday – at work and outside it – against the list of skills below. Consider aspects that have been listed for each skill (pages 13-22) and include those. For example, communication skills include listening, writing, discussing and presenting.

SKILLS PROFILE

SKILL	ASPECTS OF THE SKILL
❏ Self-awareness	_____
	_____
❏ Self-management	_____
	_____
❏ Interpersonal skills	_____
	_____
❏ Flexibility	_____
	_____
❏ Communication	_____
	_____
❏ Problem solving	_____
	_____
❏ Team-working	_____
	_____
❏ Business awareness	_____
	_____
❏ Networking	_____
	_____
❏ Negotiation	_____
	_____
❏ Leadership	_____
	_____
❏ Computer literacy	_____
	_____
❏ Language skills	_____
	_____
❏ Driving ability	_____
	_____

Once you have written down the aspects you have developed, give yourself a mark out of four for each main skill, using the scores below. Remember to take into account all the elements you have included.

1 = poor   2 = satisfactory   3 = good   4 = excellent

Check through to make sure that your final scores agree with your first analysis – and the task is complete. You have a skills profile which pinpoints the skills you have, at what level, and where you need to develop further.

Employment skills

Once you have identified the basic and transferable skills you have – and where the gaps are – you can then start to think about those extra skills you want to develop which are specific to a particular job area or function. You may want to take vocational qualifications in the industry you work in – or would like to work in, or professional exams which could take you another rung up the ladder or improve your income.

If you already know where you would like to be in three or five years' time, you are likely to have at least some idea of the sort of qualifications you might want (or need) to get you there. If you are hoping to branch into a different employment area, you'll need to do some research into what qualifications and experience are necessary.

If you want to develop where you are, you can discuss your learning needs with your human resources or personnel department, if there is one. If there isn't, ask your line manager or an outside expert such as a careers adviser. If all else fails, use the resources available to you locally such as the public library, Jobcentre or Citizens' Advice Bureau. They will be able to point you in the right direction.

If you have no idea where you want to go, you could:

▌ get some professional advice (read on to find out how and where)

▌ talk to colleagues, friends and relations

▌ do some background reading.

From there, write down:
- the employment skills you will need
- the ones you have already (any qualifications and experience)
- the gaps you need to fill.

You can use a skills profile like the one on page 28.

Extra help

Recognising and evaluating your skills can be a tricky task, even with a skills profile. It is often difficult to be objective about your own achievements – particularly if you take those attributes for granted because you use them every day.

But you can get help! You could:
- get **professional advice** – at work or outside
- ask a **friend or relative** to help
- find out about ways of **accrediting your previous experience**

The organisation and delivery of careers advice and guidance has changed dramatically over the past few years. It has been recognised that you don't just take a decision when you leave school that you'll be a teacher or a plumber and that's it, your need for careers advice is finished. In fact, quite the reverse is true. With the disappearance of a 'job for life', people are going to need more and more advice and guidance throughout their working lives for career and personal development, and this need is something that a growing number of employers are recognising.

Regular **appraisal** at work is now commonplace and serves as an effective benchmark by which to assess your current levels and plan for the future. In some organisations there are even 'competence frameworks' to help you match your skills levels more accurately to the needs of the job.

Careers services are now run by independent companies, who are keen to deliver their services to adults as well as school students. They have advisers who are trained in adult guidance and can help you plan your next steps.

Some regions offer a package of help (sometimes known as 'Gateways'), which includes assessment of your skills and psychometric testing to identify your interests and strengths. The pattern followed is usually:

1. A consultation to talk about your education and career pattern to date.
2. Psychometric testing to pinpoint your strengths and potential – and feedback on what the tests mean.
3. A return visit to discuss future steps.
4. An action plan, which you write with your adviser, detailing the steps you need to take to achieve your goals, including:
   - your existing qualifications
   - your long-term and short-term vocational goals
   - the action you need to take to achieve those goals
   - any problems that could affect your progress
   - any follow-up arrangements.

Ask careers services near you what they can provide. Contact your regional Training and Enterprise Council (TEC) or Local Enterprise Company (LEC) in Scotland for information about what is available near you. You could also visit your local library, Jobcentre or Citizens' Advice Bureau. You'll find addresses the phone book.

Colin felt he was stuck in a rut. He knew he wanted to do something different, but he didn't know what. He went along to his local careers service for advice.

'The worst of it was not knowing what I was aiming for. What else could I do? I did some tests to show up my strengths and weaknesses and we looked at suitable occupational areas that tied up with my skills, discussing the parts of my current job that I enjoy. I realised how much I enjoy the organisational side of my job, getting things done efficiently and on time. As a result, I'm going to start training with NVQs in Business Administration at work and I'm taking an open learning course too. I now realise that I do have skills and positive attributes which I can use and develop.'

As the importance of careers advice for adults is recognised, more and more flexible arrangements are being made nationwide. Exactly what is available varies from region to region, but moves are afoot to ensure that an effective service exists in all parts of the country – and that high quality is maintained. Here are just a few examples of the kinds of developments that are going on all over the country.

▌If you live in northwest Wales, you are likely to be able to tap into free careers advice and guidance in centres such as public libraries or Citizens' Advice Bureaux. You can ask the questions you need answered, such as 'Where can I take a course in computer-aided design?' 'How much will it cost?' 'What could I do with it once I'd got a qualification?' An expert will guide you through the maze to the solutions you need.

▌In the Chester/Wirral area, you can access a Learning Link in one of two public libraries. An information officer is on hand to give you information and advice and to identify a relevant organisation that can help. In addition, they have computer careers and guidance packages and reference books, which you can browse through. In two other libraries in the region you'll find display areas, leaflet racks and computers which contain details of all the education and training courses available near you. If you can't find out what you need to know, simply contact the information officer at one of the manned sites. It is also hoped to set up a mobile 'outreach' centre which will travel around to rural communities. Ring the Training and Enterprise Council in Birkenhead, for details.

▌Ashington, Northumberland, has an Information Station, a high street shop which offers a free confidential service to anyone who's unemployed. It offers free psychometric testing and help with CV preparation and advice.

Learning Direct is a new, free telephone helpline set up to answer queries on learning and careers. They can also help if you want to find out about funding your course or finding childcare while you learn. Ring on 0800 100 900. It's nationwide and won't cost you a penny.

Friends and relatives can act as great sounding-boards when it comes to working out your skills levels – as long as they're frank.

(Don't choose a friend who's going to flatter – make sure they'll tell it like it is.) With their help you should be able to moderate your own ideas of your attributes and discuss aspects that you may not have considered before. With a friend or relative who knows you well you can talk over how you perform in different situations.

Whether you are in employment at the moment or not, you probably have many more roles than you think – and they can be recognised and **accredited**. For example, you might:

■ manage the family budget
■ plan and produce regular menus and meals
■ provide childcare – for your own or other children
■ sort out maintenance problems with the house, garden or car
■ be involved in organising local events.

In all these activities you are using skills that you could apply in a job. For instance, when you choose your fruit in the market or your meat at the butcher, you are negotiating. When you run a home and children you have to be good at self-management. And above all, if you live with other people, you are likely to be displaying flexibility, interpersonal, communication and negotiation skills around the clock. And there are ways for you to get formal recognition for your achievements. Finding out how they apply to you can help you work out where the gaps still are – and how you are going to fill them.

Accreditation of Prior Learning (APL)

APL is a process that can give you credit against skills and knowledge you already have in the form of a qualification or part qualification. It is particularly useful if you have spent time out of education or work, for instance raising a family. Because APL recognises skills that already exist, the time you need to spend on any training is reduced. It means that you can achieve full qualifications more quickly than through more traditional routes – and it's likely to cost you less. You could end up with a NVQ awarded for skills you have built up over time but not recorded.

APL isn't just an easy way to qualifications – you need motivation and dedication if you are going to make your skills count this way.

THE SIX STAGES OF APL

1. **Pre-entry** – when you receive information about APL, its benefits and costs.
2. **Initial screening** – an opportunity to discuss your experiences with an APL adviser. The adviser will identify your skills and map out an action plan.
3. **Gathering and reviewing evidence** – your next step is to collect and produce evidence to prove you can do what you say you can.
4. **Assessment** – a trained assessor will look at your evidence. The assessor may ask you questions and request further information. This could involve the demonstration of a skill, for example.
5. **Accreditation** – an awarding body will then approve your qualification or credits towards it.
6. **Post-assessment guidance** – your adviser will help you develop a plan for further training or education.

To find out more about APL, contact your local college of further education and ask to meet the APL adviser, or call your local TEC or LEC to see where APL services are available near you. You'll find contact details in the local phone book.

Some colleges and universities run **Credit Accumulation and Transfer Schemes (CATS)** , where elements of a course you have done previously can count towards a qualification. Colleges and universities have the details – contact the central administration office.

National Records of Achievement (NRAs)

NRAs have been developed for everyone to use throughout their life. Currently, they're used mostly by school-leavers. NRAs are a summary record of a person's achievements, both formal and informal. They can be used at interviews for jobs and training and for planning future learning.

If you are currently on a government training scheme, such as a Modern Apprenticeship or Training for Work, you are automatically entitled to a free NRA from your local TEC (Training and Enterprise

Council). You can obtain an NRA information folder from the Department for Education and Employment, Room E4A, Moorfoot, Sheffield S1 4PQ. Tel: 0114 259 3871.

Decide whether – and how – to fill the gaps

Once you have identified the gaps in your skills, you need to decide whether you are going to fill them, which to choose first, and how you'll go about it. Whether or not to fill those gaps depends on the direction you want your life to take and what commitment you are prepared to make.

Where do you want to go?

You may be able to answer this immediately. Perhaps you have always had a burning ambition to be an engine driver or an eye surgeon, a fire fighter or a florist. Maybe you simply want to have a more fulfilling role with your current employer – or to become an employer in yourself. On the other hand, it may take months of careful analysis and discussion of your needs before you can reach a conclusion.

Write down the skills areas that you already know you'd like to develop. For example, you may want to improve your presentation skills, learn to write better reports, or get up to speed with computer technology. Or you may have been planning to learn to speak fluent French, or take some professional exams.

Now look more specifically at where you see yourself in, say, three years' time. Would you still like to be doing the same job? Perhaps you are looking for more responsibility? Would you like to change direction? Or would you just be grateful for any job? To decide on your career direction, you need to do some research into:

■ job options
■ what the work entails
■ what training you need
■ job availability.

There are plenty of people – and publications – to help you. Read more about this in Chapter 5, and take a look at some of the books listed in 'Where to find out more' (page 81). It is also worth contacting your local careers service (address in your local phone book).

Once you have completed your career direction research, write down on the worksheet below what you are aiming for – your goals. Be realistic, but at the same time aim to stretch yourself. Why not give yourself a challenge?

Filling the gaps

Having identified your goals, write down the skills you think you need for each particular goal. You may need to:

- brush up on your basic skills
- improve your transferable skills, or develop new ones
- take some qualifications.

WORK SHEET

Where I want to go – and what I need to get there

Career direction – where I see myself in three years' time

Skills needed for this role　　　　**Skills I need to develop for this role**

Basic skills

Transferable skills

Employment skills

Academic qualifications

There are a variety of ways through which you can improve your skills. You could:

- ask for experience in a particular area at work to fill a skills gap
- look for a job which would develop the skills you need
- train at work in your current role
- take a course of study
- gain experience outside work.

Gaining experience at work

It is often possible to gain the experience you are looking for by fulfilling a different role at work.

Stella worked in a clerical job in the out-patients department of a hospital. She wanted to move eventually into a negotiation role in the contracting department.

'I'd really like to play a part in developing contracts with GPs and other purchasers but I have no experience of that side of things. So I asked if I could move into the department that deals with GP fundholding for a while. Through doing that I'm learning to negotiate in a minor way as well as familiarising myself with the background. In addition, I'm able to sit in at some of the meetings to gain first-hand experience.'

Secondment is an option used by many organisations. Staff are seconded to another section, a different location or a totally different firm, for a specified period of time. Secondment provides an ideal way to develop new skills in an unfamiliar environment. It's also useful as a way of trying out a new role before taking the plunge permanently.

Ask your human resources or personnel department or your line manager about the possibilities. And read more in Chapter 5.

Finding a different job to fill the gaps

It may be worth taking a first step along the path of career change via a totally different job. Look at the goals you have set yourself. Could another job enrich your experience and be directly applicable to your aims?

CASE study

Wes wanted to join the police force but knew that his experience of dealing with the public was minimal.

'I decided to get a job in retail, dealing directly with the public, before becoming a policeman. I must say, it's been a real eye opener. It's certainly improved my communication and interpersonal skills – along with my patience levels.'

Talk to your local careers service or your human resources or personnel department for advice on jobs in other areas. Browse through the books in the careers section of your public library, and look at some of the titles suggested in 'Where to find out more', page 81.

Training at work in your current role

There is often training available at work which can improve the skills you already have and develop new ones. For example, NVQs have been developed to give recognition for the skills people actually use at work. You can train at work or college – or both. Read about NVQs in the section on Qualifications (page 48) and Chapter 5.

MODERN APPRENTICESHIPS are specifically for people of 16 and over, offering them the opportunity to gain high-level skills and qualifications, training while they work. Read more about Modern Apprenticeships in Chapter 6.

> The **Investors in People** award is a sign of quality, granted to companies who have made a commitment to investing in their staff. This includes a significant commitment to training, with the aim of producing consistently high standards.

IN-HOUSE TRAINING is offered at many workplaces, to update skills or develop new ones. Ask your human resources or personnel department or line manager for more details.

PROFESSIONAL TRAINING is available for many jobs, in areas as diverse as marketing or management, medicine or media. Professional bodies will keep you up to date about what is going on in your profession, where you need to develop skills and knowledge, and what training is available. Read more in Chapter 5.

Taking a course of learning

You can take a course in any subject you care to name, covering all skills areas. This means learning in its broadest sense – everything from the most academic of subjects to a leisure qualification such as sailing or sewing. Any learning you are involved in helps to develop important skills to improve your employability. Even attending an evening class with no certification at the end will develop skills such as self-confidence, self-reliance, communication and interpersonal skills. You can build your skills without even trying.

Before taking a course of study, you need to decide how and where you want to learn. You can learn:

- at work
- at home – or anywhere else that's convenient
- in the community
- at college
- abroad!

LEARNING AT WORK

Employee learning facilities are available at many workplaces nowadays, where you can brush up on your knowledge while you are at work. Some organisations have purpose-built Employee Learning Centres where people can drop in at agreed times (or whenever suits them), often to study open learning courses which they follow by themselves at their own pace.

LEARNING AT HOME

Learning at home usually involves a method known as open learning. It's like distance learning in that you can study at your own pace, in a place and at a time that suits you. And there are no age barriers – you can take a course whatever your age. There is usually support available from a tutor, either at the end of a phone or at a college or summer school. Some colleges have drop-in centres where people can arrange to follow 'teach yourself' courses using the college's facilities, in much the same way as employees can use an Employee Learning Centre.

Open learning study materials can be paper-based (books), computer software or audio or video cassettes. You do need to be well motivated to see the course through to the end, particularly if you are following it at home rather than with friends or colleagues at work.

CASE study

Adrian started window cleaning when he was 14 and is now managing director of his own firm of specialist cleaning contractors. However, his meteoric rise to success didn't allow him time to gain the skills he needed to run a business – nor to ensure the appropriate grounding for his staff.

'I now employ an average of ten staff and we specialise in cleaning newly built houses, office blocks, shops and factories, as well as doing jobs for estate agents, holiday camps and property owners. I realised last year that I didn't know enough about the business to fulfil all my ambitions and develop in the way I wanted to go.

'I sent off for details about open learning courses and now we're all working on elements of courses so that we can get the relevant qualifications and show our customers that we offer a high-quality service. It's taught us not just about the technical processes but also how to manage our time effectively, set objectives and achieve them – and generally run a business! Everyone feels much better motivated now and more enthusiastic – and that's an upward spiral. We couldn't have done this without open learning – the nearest college is miles away and we can't guarantee being able to spare the time to go and take part in a course on a regular basis. This way, we can work our way through the study pack as and when there's an opportunity.'

CASE study

Fiona has found that open learning has boosted her confidence.

'I got married and had children but when they'd grown up I took a job as a receptionist. Seven years ago I gave that up because of bad health and I haven't worked since. I've had very bad depressions and been less and less confident about going out there and trying to find a job, but my daughter persuaded me to try an open learning course and it's made all the difference. I was able to take it at our local community school, combining work in class with study at home.

'I was apprehensive to start with, but I've had so much support from the community centre. Six months ago I could never have talked like this about what I'm doing. Now I'm going on to take a word-processing course by open learning – I'm determined to get back to work. I've got a reason now to get up and go. Improving my skills like this has been better than a doctor's prescription for me!'

You may have heard of the following open learning providers, such as the following.

THE OPEN UNIVERSITY offers degree, diploma and certificate courses which are open to all adults. You don't need any qualifications to be accepted and anyone can apply. Places are allocated on a first come, first served basis. Students learn from TV and radio 'lectures' as well as textbooks and other materials.

Find out more from the Open University, Central Enquiries, PO Box 200, Milton Keynes MK7 6AA. Tel: 01908 274066.

FINANCIAL TIMES MANAGEMENT (previously The Open College) specialises in work-related courses covering management and supervision, health and care, technology and education and training.

The organisation also produces CD-ROMs and videos. For more information, contact: Financial Times Management, Portland Tower, Portland Street, Manchester M1 3LD. Tel: 0161 245 3300.

THE OPEN COLLEGE OF THE ARTS (OCA). Affiliated to the Open University, the OCA offers courses in creative arts such as art and design, creative writing, drawing, garden design, history of art, music, painting, photography, sculpture and textiles. As well as home study, students have back-up from tutors in various colleges of art, universities, schools, art centres, studios or in some cases by post.

Contact the Open College of the Arts, Houndhill, Worsborough, Barnsley, South Yorkshire S70 6TU. Tel: 0891 168902 (information line).

THE NATIONAL EXTENSION COLLEGE offers over 150 home study courses, including GCSEs, A-levels and an impressive range of other recognised qualifications.

Find out more from National Extension College, 18 Brooklands Avenue, Cambridge CB2 2HN. Tel: 01223 316644.

TV LEARNING: BBC, ITV and Channel 4 all transmit educational programmes for home learners. In some cases you can buy books, audio and video cassettes and other material to back up your study.

Find out more from the TV guides or contact BBC Education Information Line on 0181 746 1111, Monday to Friday, 9.30am to 5.30pm, and ask about the Learning Zone.

<table>
<tr><td>

Quicklist of some ways of learning
Full time
Part time
Evening class
Day release – one day a week from work
Block release – blocks of time spent away from work, at college
Sandwich course – college course that includes time (usually one year) on work placement

</td></tr>
</table>

LEARNING IN THE COMMUNITY

This might be an option you hadn't considered before. But the number of community-based groups is increasing all the time. You could think about:

■ self-help groups
■ skills exchanges
■ community action groups
■ campaigns, festivals and societies.

If you have children, you may go along with them to their leisure activities – such as Girl Guides or football coaching. You may even get involved in running the admin side or offering coaching. Both these (and many more) are great ways of developing your skills. Additionally you can take courses – in football coaching or business studies, for instance – which can help you. See page 63 for Employee Development Schemes, which describes people who have done just that.

LEARNING AT COLLEGE

This an option you may already know – or do you? Things are much more flexible than they used to be. Often a range of teaching methods is used, in a less formal atmosphere than the restrictive classroom environment you might envisage.

There are a number of choices. You could study at a:
■ further education/tertiary college
■ higher education college/university
■ adult residential college.

FURTHER EDUCATION AND TERTIARY COLLEGES have traditionally offered work-related (vocational) courses, mostly for young people.

But now more and more adults are taking advantage of college courses – in fact, on many courses more than half the students are 'mature students'. (That means over 25!)

For financial reasons, colleges nowadays have to be especially aware of the number of students they are attracting, so they are becoming increasingly flexible about the range of courses they offer. For example, your local agricultural college may now be offering computer studies or water-colour painting in the evenings, to bolster their revenue. Which is all good news for students!

> **English for Speakers of Other Languages (ESOL):** Many colleges and community centres run courses to help you if your first language is not English.

Some colleges run taster courses which give a sample of what a course is like. Names vary around the country, but they have titles such as Next Step, Return to Learn, Pathway, Wider Opportunities or New Directions.

Very often they not only give you an idea of what's on offer, they also combine:

- personal guidance
- confidence building
- communication skills
- information on other options.

Your local college or public library will have details.

UNIVERSITIES AND HIGHER EDUCATION COLLEGES offer advanced courses leading to degrees or Higher National Certificates or Diplomas (HNCs/HNDs).

Since universities are keen to attract mature students, the structure of many courses is changing. More and more degrees are of a **modular** nature, which means that you can do parts of the course and build them up over a period of time until you complete your degree. (Read on page 34 about CATS – Credit Accumulation and Transfer Schemes – which allow you to have separate modules from different institutions accredited. APL – Accreditation of Prior Learning – may also help with your application if you feel you are underqualified. There's more on APL on page 33.)

Childcare: Some colleges and education centres have crèche facilities or nurseries to care for small children while you study. If you are at work, there may be workplace facilities. There are also LEA or privately run nurseries, as well as out-of-school and in-school clubs for school-age children, run in school buildings after hours. Find out more about childcare by ringing Learning Direct 0800 100 900

Some universities run short courses for adults through their extra-mural or continuing education department. Still more offer **Access** courses for adults without GCSEs or A-levels who feel they may want to take a higher qualification. Access courses give you the foundations to prepare for higher education. Because the students are mature, and tend to have other responsibilities, the courses are often run on a flexible basis to fit in with outside commitments. It's a gentle way to ease you into the university environment.

Sarah hadn't worked since she got married but, with the children growing up, she wanted to fulfil her ambition to take a degree in some aspect of art and design, with a view to starting her own business.

'Early last summer, with my 50th birthday on the horizon, I heard about an Access course at the local university. Friends gave me the courage to apply and now I go along to the course two days a week, with one evening of life drawing – and around 12 hours of homework a week. I've never been to university but I've always hankered after it. And now through this course I've found the subject I'd like to study.'

Adult residential colleges offer residential courses to adults who may not have traditional educational qualifications. The course you take could lead to a place on a higher education course.

For full details of residential colleges, contact the Adult Residential Colleges Association (ARCA), Wansfell College, 30 Piercing Hill, Theydon Bois, Essex CM16 7LF; Tel: 01992 813027.

Computerised information

TAPs (Training Access Points) provide information, via an easy-to-use computer terminal, on local education and training opportunities. TAPs will tell you what's available at colleges locally or through private training providers. You'll also be able to find out details such as times, methods of study and contact names. You'll find

TAPS in some supermarkets, colleges and community centres.

ECCTIS 2000 helps you find out about university courses. It gives quick access to information on nearly 100,000 courses at over 700 universities and colleges in the UK. You can find out appropriate courses for you, how long they last, the method of study and contact names.

Learning abroad

Opting for education or training abroad means that you can develop your skills, expand your knowledge and add to your qualifications – as well as enjoying the chance to spend time in another country.

Depending on your personal circumstances and skill development needs, you could:

- incorporate a course as part of a break away
- spend time abroad at a university or college
- take advantage of a training opportunity or placement
- sample a study holiday, where you live with a family.

It's a great way to add to your CV and develop employment skills, but you need to check out:

- tuition costs
- residency laws
- the country's higher education system.

There are courses at all levels and for any duration – from just a few days to a full undergraduate degree programme (usually taught in the first language of that country). If you are already a graduate, you could apply for a place at the European University Institute in Florence or the College of Europe in Bruges. They're two of the best-known postgraduate institutions, offering one-year MA courses and three-year doctoral degrees which specifically relate to European studies. See some of the publications listed in 'Where to find out more' (page 81) for details.

Or what about spending time studying in the United States? The Council on International Educational Exchange (CIEE) organises study abroad programmes. Contact CIEE on 0171 706 3008.

Gaining experience outside work

Volunteering is another way of learning in the community that will extend and develop your skills. It could involve anything from working with disabled children, to organising a 'fun run' to raise money for a worthy cause, to running your local Brownie pack.

Whether or not you are already in a job, there are plenty of opportunities for you to volunteer – either locally or further afield. Read more about this in Chapters 5 and 7.

Many companies nowadays have their own schemes whereby employees put something back into their local community. These are a perfect way to develop skills such as communication, team-work, leadership and interpersonal skills. You can find out more about such schemes in Chapter 5.

In brief

- identify the skills you already have (and at what level)
- work out your skills gaps
- decide whether and how to fill the gaps.

4 Developing your skills

Once you have identified your skills and decided which gaps to fill, how do you go about it? Read first about the qualifications that are available, and choose which might be the right ones for you. The second half of the chapter describes how to make an action plan and how to ensure that your plan works for you.

Qualifications – a brief guide

GCE A-levels and AS qualifications

(GCE A-level – General Certificate of Education, Advanced level. AS – Advanced Supplementary.) These are academically demanding two-year courses, available in a wide range of subjects. An AS is half the content of an A-level, but at the same standard. Many courses now are modular, with continuous assessment.

GNVQ/GSVQs – General National/Scottish Vocational Qualifications

Mainly for young people in full-time education, but sometimes courses may be offered part time.

GNVQ/GSVQs are available at three levels:

- An **Advanced GNVQ/GSVQ** broadly equals two A-levels, normally take two years and doesn't require any previous qualifications.
- An **Intermediate** GNVQ/GSVQ broadly equals at least four GCSEs at grades A★–C, normally takes one year and doesn't require any previous qualifications.
- A **Foundation** GNVQ/GSVQ broadly equals four GCSEs at grades D–G, normally takes one year and doesn't require any previous qualifications.

Gained unit by unit, GNVQ/GSVQs prepare you for a range of jobs or for further study. They are offered by awarding bodies including Edexcel Foundation, C&G (City and Guilds) and the RSA (RSA Examinations Board). GNVQ and NVQs are gradually replacing the old-style qualifications offered by these awarding bodies.

GNVQ/GSVQs subjects include: Art & Design, Business, Construction & Built Environment, Engineering, Health & Social Care, Hospitality & Catering, Information Technology, Leisure & Tourism, Management Studies, Manufacturing, Retail & Distributive Services, Media: Communication & Production, Science.

NVQ/SVQs – National/Scottish Vocational Qualifications

Mainly for people already in work or work-based training, NVQ/SVQs comprise units which are assessed in working conditions.

NVQ levels range from 1–5 and relate to:

- Foundation level (level 1) – NVQ/SVQ level 1, equivalent to four or more GCSEs at grades D–G.
- Intermediate level (level 2) – NVQ/SVQ level 2, equivalent to four or more GCSEs at grades A★–C.
- Advanced level (level 3) – NVQ/SVQ level 3, equivalent to two GCE A-levels.
- Levels 4 and 5 – NVQ/SVQ levels 4 and 5, equivalent to a degree or Higher National Diploma (HND).

You can take an NVQ/SVQ part time as part of a job or training, in the evening or full time. They are available in most work areas and are offered by awarding bodies including Edexcel Foundation, C&G, the RSA, CITB (the Construction Industry Training Board) and EnTRA (the Engineering Training Authority).

Other job-related qualifications

Edexcel, C&G, the RSA Examinations Board and many other vocational awarding bodies award other qualifications as well as NVQ/SVQs and GNVQ/SNVQs.

Edexcel and C&G qualifications are popular in subjects such as business and finance, leisure and tourism, engineering, catering and caring.

- BTEC Nationals – normally take two years.
- BTEC Higher Nationals – normally take two years.
- BTEC Awards – a combination of units from any BTEC qualifications – normally take one or two years.
- BTEC Nationals usually require four GCSEs (grades A*–C) or a qualification equal to this. BTEC Higher Nationals usually require a BTEC National or one A-level. BTEC Awards don't require any previous qualifications.

RSA qualifications are most popular in subjects such as information technology (IT), word-processing and typing, retailing and languages.

- There are C&G and RSA courses available at most levels.
- Some short RSA courses develop skills which are useful at all levels, such as IT and word-processing.
- Levels 1 and 2 usually require no previous qualifications.
- To take level 3 you usually need a level 2 qualification.
- For a short RSA course you may need to provide proof of your achievements at lower levels.

Higher education courses

- BA (Bachelor of Arts) and BSc (Bachelor of Science) are first degree, or undergraduate, courses. They usually take three or four years, sometimes including a sandwich year in a work placement.
- Masters degrees are postgraduate courses of higher education, usually taking two years.
- MBA – Master of Business Administration – usually one or two years (or can be longer part time), increasingly important in the world of business.
- Doctorates – postgraduate research qualifications.

Read more about how to choose and use these qualifications in the following chapters.

Larry followed an MBA programme – and it changed his future.

'I felt an MBA was essential for my career progression. So much variety was offered on the programme that I found it an ideal way to prepare for general management and gain experience through networking with people in other industries. I studied part time while still working, applying what I learned in college to my job every day of the week. The calibre of participants and lecturers has been such that it's like seeing a microcosm of what occurs in reality, allowing you to analyse situations from a different level of experience and problem solve in unfamiliar situations. As a result of the MBA I've been offered an important developmental role within the company, which promises an exciting time ahead.'

Comparing the different qualifications

General education qualifications (such as GCSEs and GCE A-levels) GNVQ/GSVQs and NVQ/SVQs can be taken at different levels.

You will reach Foundation level (level 1) when you get either:
4 or more GCSEs   Foundation GNVQ/GSVQ   NVQ level 1
at grades D–G

You will reach Intermediate level (level 2) when you get either:
4 or more GCSEs   Intermediate GNVQ/GSVQ   NVQ level 2
at grades A–C

You will reach Advanced level (level 3) when you get either:
2 GCE A-levels   Advanced GNVQ/GSVQ   NVQ level 3
(or 1 A-level and 2
AS qualifications or 4 ASs)

You will reach levels 4 and 5 with higher qualifications when you get either:
A degree   Higher National Diploma (HND)   higher professional qualifications (NVQ/SVQ levels 4 and 5)

Work out a plan of action

Statistics show that people who write down their aims and ambitions are many times more likely to achieve them than people who don't.

It's a way of helping you to keep on track towards the targets you set yourself for your life and your work. Think of the number of times you have decided to do something and then not quite got around to it – not just major events in your life, but anything from reading a book that someone recommended, to sorting through the piles of paper that seem to accumulate. It's the 'don't do today what you can put off till tomorrow' philosophy, and it's something that most of us suffer from.

It often takes a crisis in our lives to propel us into some sort of self-evaluation. Where am I going? What do I want to get out of life? What do I hope to achieve? More often than not a time of crisis is the very time when we shouldn't be making important decisions that will change our lives dramatically. Domestic problems, the threat of unemployment, bereavement, are all likely to precipitate a major rethink, and that could involve job searching and self-development activities which would be far more effective without the parapher-nalia of anxiety and stress surrounding them.

So what's the solution? If you can, take the opportunity to reflect on your life and your self-development when times are calmer and you can be more objective in your assessment and conclusions. From that starting point you are more likely to be able to build a firm grounding of skills which will give you the kind of employability you want to meet your needs.

If you make yourself an action plan, it will help you:

- formulate your aims
- focus on your goals
- chart your progress.

What's more, you are far more likely to gain satisfaction from being able to tick off your achievements as you go along.

An action plan will not only act as a memory jogger and a spur to encourage you to keep to your plans, you can also use it to learn:

- more about yourself
- more about jobs – either in your current role or elsewhere
- more about the organisation you work for, or would like to work for.

It can be a tool to help you develop more confidence in your ability to tackle new challenges and become more employable. And that's likely to lead you to getting more out of life – fast.

The main elements in the construction of your plan (and its use from now on) are:

- assessing your skills, knowledge and experience, your values and your interests. That also means being able to pinpoint your strengths and weaknesses (read how to write your own skills profile on page 28)
- understanding the opportunities that are available to you to improve your performance and develop skills – either in your current job or elsewhere – and knowing how to take advantage of them
- being able to identify possible career moves and job openings, understanding their skill requirements and the doors they might open
- understanding how to access education and training opportunities
- formulating plans for your career and skills development
- carrying out those plans – and that involves managing change in your life and coping with set-backs as you move to new roles and opportunities.

Clement spent more than 35 years with a large organisation in the motor industry and wasn't unhappy to take an early redundancy package from his job as a senior manager. But, to his consternation, he didn't find retirement easy to handle.

'My wife used to say I'd been married to the company for all those years, and I must say that when it came, leaving was a terrible wrench. I'd pictured myself playing golf all day but I found I didn't really enjoy playing by myself – I'm much more of a social animal. I needed something to do with my time.'

Clement started to apply for jobs but was told he was over qualified.

'I was willing to take a vast cut in salary but people still weren't interested. I even got turned down for a job as a school caretaker – my morale was at an all-time low then. But I went along to the local careers service and they helped put me back on my feet. The careers adviser asked me how I would tackle the situation if it were a business problem. I said I'd work out my mission statement, stating where I was heading, and then I'd work out a business plan to show how I'd get there. He just said "Exactly!" and we took it from there.

'I worked through some psychometric tests which showed that I liked working with people, helping them through difficulties. We talked about my using my training expertise and started to formulate an action plan. I became much more focused and worked out where I was going – and how. Once I'd seen my potential I realised there was no need to panic. It gave me the confidence I needed to go out and get the job I wanted. I now work one day and one evening a week as an examiner for the industry's accreditation course, as well as lecturing part time at the local college.'

Getting started with an action plan

Don't rush into writing your action plan. You have already spent time identifying skills gaps and thought about where you want to go. Now think carefully around the subject and make sure you are happy that you are setting realistic goals which will help you reach your targets. There is no point in setting yourself a goal which sounds as though it's what you'd like to do (eg be a brain surgeon, earn a six-figure salary) if it's not achievable. There is nothing more certain to make you give up – almost before you have begun.

Instead, make sure you set targets which:

▌ you want to meet
▌ will stretch your abilities (mentally, physically, or both)
▌ you know you could achieve.

Look back at Chapter 3 about how and where you could learn, and work out what is really going to suit you best.

▌ What situations have prompted you to learn in the past?
▌ What will ensure that you don't give up?
▌ Are you planning these steps as a means to an end (eg improving your employability) or because you like the idea of a challenge?
▌ Do you have responsibilities which limit the time or place you could study?
▌ How important is it to you that you have support from your family or friends in this?

- Are you so tired at the end of the day that an evening class is out of the question?
- Could you reorganise your life so that you had a regular slot each day or week which you could put aside for your personal skills development?

Lack of time and energy are the two most common reasons why people never get around to learning. By working out when and how you learn best you can maximise the opportunities you have and make them work much more effectively for you.

> Caroline found that working in the centre of London does have its advantages, despite daily commuting. She wanted to take a course to enhance her career but she knew that by the time she'd travelled home to the suburbs she would never have the energy to go out again to college.

'I found out about evening classes just around the corner from where I work. Instead of battling home immediately after a day's work I now have a snack with a friend and then we both go off to our course. Instead of its being a chore, we're finding that the change of scene revitalises us at the end of the day. It's stimulating, but because it's so different from our daily work it's actually fun! By the time we're ready to go home, the rush hour's over and the journey is much less fraught. It's certainly working well for us. I feel really refreshed by the time I set out for home. I'm hoping to do a management training course next year. It's given me a sense of achievement – and motivated me.'

You can make up your own action plan framework to suit your needs, or you can use an existing pattern and slot your goals into that. You can get expert help from your local careers service, and there may be facilities for career or individual personal development planning at your place of work.

Make it happen! is the title of the Royal Society of Arts' (RSA) Personal Learning Action Plan (PLAN) which it launched in early summer 1996. It's a clear and simple guide which anyone can use to chart their intentions. Using a step-by-step approach, the booklet:

- helps you look at your own life

- helps you set goals for the future
- shows how learning can help you achieve those goals.

There are three key stages:
1. Getting Started – thinking about why you might have learned in the past and where you are now.
2. Making your PLAN – looking at what you have learned, what you want to 'be', and how you can start to achieve your full potential.
3. Keeping Going – reviewing and updating your PLAN.

The RSA suggests creating a Personal Learning Action Plan in just five steps:

Step 1 – Taking stock of what you have already done, what learning you already have in your 'learning account'.

Step 2 – Identifying your goals in your 'wish list'.

Step 3 – Setting yourself targets in your 'hit list'.

Step 4 – Reviewing who or what has helped or hindered your past learning in your 'help account'.

Step 5 – Making your PLAN of action.

The booklet takes you through each of these stages, offering prompts to help you add flesh to the bones of your PLAN.

Organisations are being encouraged to use the PLAN as part of a company strategy to encourage employees to improve their skills and become involved in lifelong learning.

Stick to your plan

Use your action plan – and constantly review it

An action plan should never be 'set in stone'. Your goals now may well be quite different from your goals in two years' time – but that doesn't matter. What's important is that you set yourself these aims and work towards achieving them.

If as you go along you decide that you should change direction or modify your strategies, that's fine. Simply go through the planning process again, ensuring that the path you intend to take will fulfil your needs, and alter your action plan accordingly. As long as you don't abandon your action plan altogether, you will still be developing in the right direction. It's an organic process – don't give up.

Most people need some degree of support – from family, friends or colleagues – to embark on a programme of action and stick to it. Taking a course of study, for example, can be very disruptive to a family. If you are the one who normally prepares the evening meal and studying is going to change all that, it's going to be a steep learning curve for everyone involved.

If taking an open learning course at home means covering the table with books every night or shutting yourself away for hours on end, you need to make sure that everyone understands the implications and appreciates the support you are going to need. It's important to sort out the potential problems sooner rather than later.

Enlist the support or encouragement of a friend or relative if you think that will help you through. They could become your mentor. This can be almost anyone who is willing to act as a 'sounding board' when you explore ideas, challenging and encouraging you – often in equal measure. Your mentor can help you devise an action plan (preferably with a timescale), which will lead you to your goals. It's then the mentor's role to cajole you to stick to it.

Mentors are useful when you are not sure about your abilities or aims. They can help you decide what your attributes are and where you need to brush up on your skills. And they're allowed to be (and should be) totally honest! Typically, a mentor could be: a colleague; a former teacher or adviser or a friend.

It sounds a rather onerous and responsible task, but mentoring is usually done on a very informal basis – a cup of coffee and a chat rather than a formal interview. Choosing to have a mentor is a way of making sure that you stick to what you say you are going to do, and of knowing that there's someone who takes an interest in what you are doing – and can be objective.

If you find that you have ground to a halt and you are no longer making any progress towards your goals, reassess the situation and ask yourself why.

- Did you ask too much of yourself, setting yourself unrealistic goals?
- Were you convinced deep down that you just didn't have the ability to succeed?
- Did you find that, when it came to the crunch, your motivation was too low and you just couldn't be bothered to carry on?
- Were the openings and opportunities simply not there?

Once you have identified the reasons, you can start to rethink your approach, address the causes and adjust your goals.

In brief

- work out a plan of action
- stick to it!

5 In employment?

The world of work is moving faster than ever, and we all have to move with the times if we are to stay in employment. Whether you are going to be dragged kicking and screaming into the 21st century or bound into it with enthusiasm, for sustained success in your working life, you must be prepared to develop your employment skills – even if you are already in employment. Making sure you develop yourself will not only bring more personal and job satisfaction, it will also improve your career progression prospects.

For many people, learning is something they were glad to leave behind on their last day of school. There's no doubt about it, if school didn't go well for you, you'll probably carry negative memories into your adult life. You are also likely to be more reluctant – and find it more difficult – to take any new learning on board.

The workplace, however, has the potential to break down barriers to learning, wiping away prejudices about what learning is like and what it's for. It can offer a 'safe' environment where you can learn with the support of other people.

Employers now need more people who can offer brain power rather than purely skills in operating specific pieces of equipment. Those processes which do require physical and manual skills are likely to demand skill levels which can now be recognised through qualifications, ensuring high standards for the employer and higher satisfaction for the employee. Developing individual employees and tapping their potential is therefore being placed much higher up many employers' agendas.

There are a range of ways in which you can develop your skills while you are in employment. You could:

■ gain accreditation for knowledge and skills you already use in your job

- update or improve your professional expertise
- take another course of study to reach a goal
- take part in an employee development scheme
- get involved in a community action programme.

Gain accreditation for knowledge and skills

National and Scottish Vocational Qualifications (NVQ/SVQs) are available now for nearly 90% of the workforce. Although they can be followed at college, supported by work experience, NVQs are mainly for people already in work or work-based training. They are made up of units which relate to the tasks carried out at work, and are assessed in working conditions.

NVQ/SVQs are based on the recognition of the skills you use at work and are most likely to be accredited by the professional body relating to that area of work. These vocational qualifications are available at some levels in almost all areas of work. There is normally a range of programmes available at different levels, seen increasingly as a way of raising skill levels and improving competence. New qualifications are being accredited all the time by the industry lead bodies, which set standards for each industry. (See page 48 for details on NVQ/SVQ levels and how you can take them.)

People are finding that having their skills and knowledge accredited with an NVQ/SVQ gives them the satisfaction of knowing that they are attaining national quality standards, as well as a qualification which they could take with them to other employers.

Maria was a physiotherapy helper who, despite her years of experience, both in work and running a home, had nothing on paper to confirm her competence.

'I'd worked on and off since leaving school, been well trained but had nothing to show for it on paper, so I went to local the careers service for guidance and they explained about NVQs. Three of us at work took up the challenge. We started building up our portfolios of evidence so that they could be assessed. It took a great deal of writing about every aspect of the job. Although it covered everyday work, it sometimes pointed up areas where we felt we needed a bit more information or some retraining. We filled in those gaps and as a result now feel much more competent at our jobs.

'We finally submitted our portfolios, were interviewed about them by the assessor and were awarded NVQ level 3 in Mobility and Movement. It was great to be presented with the certificate at the end. I got a real sense of achievement from being given my first piece of paper which shows that I can do a job well.

'I think you can become very complacent when you do a job year in, year out. NVQs are an excellent way of improving standards. I certainly feel better motivated now and have greater job satisfaction. It's made me think about where I'm going and what I want out of my life. One of the biggest benefits is that I've got more responsibility now and have the chance to pull my own strings a bit more – all that hard work and dedication has definitely paid off.'

Maria also had her previous skills recognised through APL (Accreditation of Prior Learning). Read about it on page 33.

Improve professional expertise

If you want to improve or update your professional skills, but NVQs aren't necessarily what you are looking for, you could turn to a **professional organisation**. You may think that professional bodies exist to promote their profession, if you think about them at all. That is certainly their prime purpose, but fundamental to that is the achievement and maintenance of high standards, involving keeping members up to date and informed, developing national standards, and promoting professional qualifications. They also have a vital role in helping their members develop the skills they need, not only to maintain high standards, but also to ensure that they continue to succeed.

Professional bodies come in all shapes and sizes, but each offers a service to its members and the opportunity for them to gain recognition for their professional status. Using the services they offer, you can recognise the skills and knowledge you need in your profession, identify gaps and take steps to build up your skills profile so that it meets the demands of a competitive work environment and ensures your employability.

An increasing number of professional organisations now:

▌ identify skills needs and prescribe professional standards
▌ provide ways for you to attain these goals, through:
　– offering courses or qualifications themselves

In employment? **69**

– signposting you to relevant training

– giving details of publications that can help.

Many professional organisations publish information specifically on skills areas within their field, such as books on how to deal with a range of scenarios, or skills checklists. Many have well-stocked libraries which members can access, including trade journals and CD-ROM. Internet information is also under development. **Resource centres** usually pride themselves on a fast response to requests for information on techniques, skills and innovations.

You can access help from the relevant professional organisation whether you are updating existing skills, acquiring new ones, or going for a nationally recognised qualification. They will tell you what you need to achieve and may offer you a range of courses to choose from. **Short courses** may be available, usually lasting between one day and a week, and dealing with specific aspects such as personal skills and effectiveness, group presentations, negotiation and decision making, time management, problem solving and coping with stress. Often you'll find that they take place at a regional centre, within easy travelling distance.

Many professional bodies accredit programmes of **professional training**, award national qualifications and deliver programmes to achieve them. As national standards become more and more important in all professional areas, so it is the professional bodies that work towards building the framework, specifying the skills needed and identifying routes to their attainment. And, recognising the demands made on employees nowadays, they provide a range of support services to help you.

Some professional bodies require members to have passed their own professional exams, which may involve you in a programme of self-study lasting several years. Throughout the period of training and education, however, you will be able to access support, such as:

∎ career and skills counselling

∎ student advisers

∎ a network of regional branches.

Many professional bodies have also developed their own processes to provide a framework for members to profile their development and achieve their goals. Programmes like these come in a variety of guises and with a selection of titles, such as Professional Development Scheme, Continuing Professional Education and Continuing Professional Development.

Your professional organisation will be able to give you details of its programmes and the form that they take. (Read more about career development on pages 65–66.)

Take another course of study

You may decide you want to take a course at college to fulfil your aims, or study by distance learning. What about taking an A-level or GCSE – in languages or business studies, for instance – or following an Edexcel or City and Guilds programme? Read on pages 47–49 about the range of qualifications you could take – and the different ways of studying.

Ramesh has started a Foundation level course in computing at his local university.

'The course is two evenings a week, for three and four hours respectively, so it's quite hard work. In addition, there are assignments, research and projects to be completed at home, and deadlines to be met. It's pretty tough going, but it's all part of my action plan. I'm aiming after this course to take the degree. And with technology moving so rapidly at work at the moment and the job situation getting tougher, the qualifications, experience and knowledge I'll gain should improve my job prospects and give me greater opportunities for promotion. It will benefit both me and the company.'

Employee development schemes

Most organisations nowadays recognise that if they invest in their employees there will be benefits all round – a skilled and more effective workforce who have increased confidence and job satisfaction.

That is why many organisations are setting up employee development schemes. It doesn't usually matter what you choose to learn, the choice is yours. Often you can learn with friends and colleagues, sometimes at work, so you don't have to face going back into a classroom. Best of all, though, your employer pays for at least part of the cost of the course!

Not only can such a scheme offer you a way forward along a development path you have already identified, it can also be a way of easing yourself back into learning if you are apprehensive or fearful of failure. People have found that, even if they start with a purely leisure-related course such as flower arranging or golf lessons, they get the learning bug and want to go on to more. That next step is quite likely to be related to career or personal skills development.

When Louise started her graphic design course it wasn't long before she realised that it didn't suit her. She left and found work on the assembly line of an electronics manufacturer. But she knew she wanted to broaden her future possibilities.

'I just felt that if I could understand the physics behind the processes I'm involved in, it would really help me. So, when I heard about the company's employee development scheme I took the opportunity to start a City & Guilds Certificate in Basic Electrical Engineering, using open learning as a method of study to fit in with my shifts. This way I can work at my own pace – it's ideal. I've become very self-motivated again and ambitious – I hope to complete this course within six months and then move on to the Advanced level and from there to a Diploma. Not only will the course teach me what I want to know, but I'll also get a qualification which will help in my future career. I feel I'm achieving rather than letting life slip by.'

Community action programmes

There is an increasing emphasis on the role organisations play within the community. Many companies recognise that if their business is to thrive they need to have the support of the community around them. They're aware that they will reap what they sow, so they need to be prepared to contribute before they can be sure of a pay-back.

Recent MORI surveys, for instance, showed that:

- 56% of consumers prefer to buy from a company they know has a strong record of community involvement

- 59% of employees prefer to work for a company they know is involved in the community.

There are all kinds of ways in which organisations are getting involved in local communities, not just by donating cash but also by offering their expertise, their premises and their manpower. It's a great way to build up a range of skills which will help you develop in the direction you have identified. Below are just some examples of community involvement.

> **Some ways to get involved through work:**
> - Education/business partnership
> - Secondment
> - Employee volunteering
> - Provision of staff time and expertise
> - Organising fundraising events.

At **Royal Mail**, each division has a Community Action Manager to encourage groups of employees to get together, with their own community as the focal point. There are literally hundreds of projects on the go – such as a school governor training programme for employees, training for employees who want to become Young Enterprise advisers, and a one-day 'Postman's Masterclass' for postmen involved in school visits, covering aspects such as presentation skills and use of available resources.

The **Benefits Agency** has a project that involves staff taking young people with learning difficulties on practical work experience in the office. It has proved to be an effective way for staff to learn new ways of delivering training and communication, as well as developing team spirit and a wider understanding.

BET sponsors the Foyer Federation, which was set up to provide young people with opportunities to obtain both a roof over their heads and employment. BET also provides management consultancy to the Foyers on the ground, with a national network of some 50 people attached to local Foyers and working with young people.

Use a career development plan

Read in Chapter 3 about how to:
- assess your skills levels
- identify your skills needs
- plan to plug the gaps.

You may find that your employer offers a career development programme, a structured way of planning for your future. Career development plans are normally linked to an appraisal process, where your line manager or human resources representative talks through with you (usually annually) your performance in the recent past, identifying problems and setting new goals and targets for your development. As part of this process you can discuss career prospects and new directions, working out ways to ensure that you are clued up about the skills and knowledge you need in your current job and any prospective future role.

Remember – it always helps to write down your plan and periodically review it to make sure that you are keeping in line with the goals you have set (or that you move the goalposts as your needs develop).

Structured personal development is increasingly important as the 'job for life' disappears and people need to be better self-directed. It is becoming crucial that you think about your career direction, analyse professional needs and plug skills gaps.

> **Changing direction?**
> If you are in employment but thinking of changing career direction completely, you need to find out:
> • what skills you need for your new line of work
> • how to bridge your skill gaps.
> Read Chapter 3 to find out how to go about it.

In brief

You could:

- gain accreditation for knowledge and skills you already use in your job
- update/improve your professional expertise
- take another course of study to reach a goal
- take part in an employee development scheme
- chart your aims via a career development plan
- get involved in a community action programme.

Look back at previous chapters to refresh your memory about how to identify your skills needs – and what you could do to meet them.

6 Looking for a job?

Unemployment can be a stressful and demoralising time, but focusing your aims can help you through the process, on to the road to work. When you are looking for a job, you must first identify the skills you are going to need, the ones you have already, and those you have to develop. Read how in Chapter 3. Even if you think that you are sufficiently well qualified for a job and don't need to upgrade your skills, it's as well to reconsider.

When you are applying for a job, not only do you need to fulfil the academic requirements and the vocational and practical experience specified by the employer, you will also boost your chances if you can 'go the extra mile' and:

■ demonstrate your personal transferable skills
■ offer additional skills, over and above the basic requirements.

Profile your own skills levels as described in Chapter 3. Where are you lacking? Which skills are particularly strong and could be exploited? Write down your wants and needs – and ways of achieving them – in your personal action plan. Consider the demands of the job area you have in mind and identify skills from those listed earlier which would give that added extra. Think about getting some experience through volunteering. Read more about it in Chapter 7.

Getting help

It is always a good idea to access the professional help that's available to you locally, to help you focus your ideas and plan a campaign of action. Read about the help you can get on pages 30–33, and call in at the Jobcentre, which will offer you advice and tell you about specific schemes to help you get back to work.

After being made redundant for the second time, Kamlesh realised that she was lacking direction. She went along to see a careers adviser to get professional help.

'I'd started applying for jobs but felt I wasn't really making any personal progress. I'd worked in the retail industry and enjoyed it, but I didn't know whether that was the best way forward for me. The adviser talked me through my life – my qualifications, past career and personal ambitions. It was only really then that I thought about giving my life some structure. I wished I'd been more tactical in my previous decisions.

'I did a psychometric test, which gave the adviser a better idea of my potential and ability and showed up possibilities for the future. It also gave me a real insight into my own strengths and weaknesses and made me think about areas I might like to pursue. And, since the test results are in writing, I can now go to an interview and produce evidence of where my talents lie. The test showed that I have good skills in reasoning, awareness and confidence – and that alone has boosted my self-esteem and given me hope for the future.'

Need to train – or retrain?

You may find that you need to retrain for an area of work, or learn new skills. If so, there is help available.

Training for Work is the government's adult training programme, designed to help long-term unemployed people get jobs through training and work experience. The programmes can last from a month to a year or more. Time may be spent on a project, a placement with a local employer or on a training course. Training for Work is generally available to people who have been out of work for six months or more, but there is immediate entry for the following:

- people with disabilities
- those needing basic literacy/numeracy training, including English or Welsh for speakers of other languages
- anyone made redundant in a large-scale redundancy
- 18–24-year-olds, unemployed for two years or more.

There's specific help if you are disabled and want to find work. Read about it in Chapter 8.

It is also available if you are returning to the job market after a gap of two years or more for domestic reasons.

The National Council for One Parent Families (NCOPF) runs Return to Work courses and Threshold, a project to help create new opportunities for single parents who want to return to work. It also publishes *Returning to Work*, a guide for one parent families.

Choose your employer carefully – to build your skills

When looking for a job, it is always worth doing some additional research to find out the sort of education and training opportunities you'll be able to access with specific employers.

INVESTING IN PEOPLE: Many companies, of all sizes and from every sector, are working towards the Investors in People standard. That means that they have to make a commitment towards training and developing their employees.

Achieving the Investors in People standard shows that a company recognises that its people are its biggest asset – and is prepared to invest in them. It's worth finding out whether an organisation is an Investor in People.

Good companies value training and career development highly, recognising that once they've employed people with the right skills they need to invest in them to ensure that they stay that way. Some organisations will have structured training plans, designed to keep your skills up to date. Others will have more ad hoc opportunities which staff can tap into to meet particular needs.

When you are looking for employment, then, it's not just a case of assessing the skills you can offer an employer. You also need to check out what they can do for you.

MODERN APPRENTICESHIPS are the new route to jobs at technician, craft and junior management level if you are a young person over 16. They are a way of learning the key skills of an industry and gaining nationally recognised qualifications while you earn a wage.

A Modern Apprenticeship offers:

■ high quality training, lasting around three years
■ training to at least NVQ level 3
■ a training agreement with your employer
■ the opportunity to progress to higher level NVQs or higher level education at university or college
■ the development of skills such as team-work, communication and problem solving.

Modern Apprenticeships are available in over 50 industries. You can ask your local careers service for details.

Austin has a Modern Apprenticeship in the polymer industry – and already he's seeing the benefits.

'My Modern Apprenticeship has taught me a range of practical skills and given me a wide introduction to the engineering industry. I don't expect to have the same job all my working life so the skills and qualifications I gain will help me later on. I'm about to start my second year taking National Vocational Qualifications.

'I'm working towards an NVQ level 3 in both general engineering and polymer processing. These qualifications are very important to me, not only in learning about the job but also in gaining the knowledge, skills and experience to further my career. My training plan sets out what I need to be trained in and shows my progress towards my two NVQs. I hope my Modern Apprenticeship is a springboard to a successful career.'

Other training opportunities for young people, leading to nationally recognised qualifications, are available throughout the country.

Thinking about self-employment?

It could be that you have decided to work for yourself. What employment skills will you need? As well as many of those already described, you need to be able to cope with:

■ long hours
■ financial insecurity
■ living with risk

- taking the responsibility
- isolation.

You'll need to ensure that you have polished the skills that relate to dealing with other people – as organisations reduce in size some services are being axed in-house and are contracted out to smaller businesses. As a supplier, you would need to be able to produce a high-quality, reliable and competitive service.

You need to:
- plan carefully before you embark on setting up a business
- get expert advice
- make sure you are sufficiently committed and determined to succeed.

There is plenty of advice and training around to help. Ask your local TEC or Jobcentre for details. And look in your local press for information on courses which will develop the skills you need for self-employment.

In brief

- be prepared to 'go the extra mile' with the skills you can offer – think about voluntary work
- access professional help and advice
- find out about schemes that can help
- look at jobs – and employers – that offer skills training.

CHAPTER 7

Not looking for paid employment?

Even if you are not looking for paid employment at the moment, it's still a good idea to develop your employment skills. Not only is it a way of ensuring that you exercise your brain, it also helps the rest of your life run more smoothly. As a practical example, look back at the skills list on page 12 and run through the skills you need in your daily life. Think how often you are called upon to use skills such as negotiation, listening, presentation and so on.

CASE study

Darren had a long-running dispute with the neighbours, which he was finding impossible to sort out. They'd reached stalemate. Some coaching in negotiation skills helped him solve the problem.

'I was at my wits end and didn't know what to do next. I'd tried talking to them but they just didn't seem to want to listen to reason – and I was finding it hard not to lose my temper. I heard about a one-day skills course, run locally, and decided to go along. The emphasis was on negotiating – learning how to get into a 'win-win' situation, where everyone feels happy with the outcome. I tried out the techniques I'd learned on the neighbours and we gradually made progress. We may never be the best of friends, but I think we'll be able to smooth over the troubles in the end.'

Volunteering

Undertaking some voluntary work is an excellent way of building up skills – and increasing your employability.

A recent study of employers (the Industry in Business report, *Towards Employability*) showed that many young people lack the social skills necessary to become successful employees. It indicated that many employers view young people as lacking skills such as initiative, motivation, self-discipline and the ability to communicate effectively.

In response, Community Survey Volunteers (CSV) commissioned a survey which shows that businesses acknowledge that volunteering can help people gain these essential skills.

More than 75% of human resources directors of the UK's top 500 companies surveyed believed that a candidate who listed volunteering on an application form had above average:

■ self-confidence
■ teamwork skills
■ communication skills

and would be likely to bring these to the workplace.

There are many voluntary organisations around the country that are crying out for help from volunteers. You could work in a range of settings, from on the streets with homeless young people, to living in a community for people with learning difficulties, to selling goods in your local charity shop.

It is not always an easy experience – but it's certainly a challenge that will offer you an insight into other aspects of life, teach you a lot about yourself and develop skills you never dreamed you had.

8 Disabled?

If you have a disability that affects your ability to work, it is worth contacting the Jobcentre, which will put you in touch with the **Disability Employment Adviser** (DEA). The DEA is part of the **PACT** (the Placing, Assessment and Counselling Team) – which is a group made up of professionals who can offer advice and support to help you assess your abilities and skills and plan your next steps.

If you are recently disabled or are looking for a career change, the DEA can help you find a new direction.

Developing your skills

Local colleges and universities may have a wide range of courses – but are they accessible if you have a disability? Many colleges now have advisers particularly for students with disabilities, and some offer other kinds of extra support, including special training courses for disabled people.

You may find that open learning suits you better (see page 39). It allows you to learn at your own pace and in your own time, wherever is most convenient for you. That could be at a college, in your workplace, or in your own home. What's more, there's support available to you from a tutor.

> **Support at work**
> There are grants and allowances which may be available to you to provide a support worker – if you are visually impaired, for instance, or have a hearing difficulty. You may also be eligible for financial help. *Ask the Disability Employment Adviser for details.*

If you need to update your skills or learn new ones, contact the Training and Enterprise Council (TEC) near you (LEC in Scotland) to find out what support services are available.

Other sources of help

■ **SKILL: the National Bureau for Students with Disabilities**
provides an information service for disabled graduates. SKILL has a
national network of regional groups who regularly organise events
and conferences. The organisation works with universities, employers,
other voluntary agencies and publishers to create and promote
opportunities for graduates with disabilities.

■ **Residential courses for people with disabilities** – several
organisations such as the Royal National Institute for the Blind, the
Royal National Institute for Deaf People and SCOPE (for People
with Cerebral Palsy – formerly the Spastics Society) run residential
courses and training designed for people with specific disabilities. The
DEA at the Jobcentre will be able to give you details.

CASE study

*Gerry was born with spina bifida and is paralysed from the
waist down. He's following an open learning course to improve
his skills levels.*

'I work for a major manufacturing firm, on circuit fault diagnosis, and the job
suits me very well. The company supplies the computer hardware and I work
from 9 until 4.30 each day, typing in fault information. My department boss
suggested I take a Communication course to improve my skills and future
job prospects. It's a very interesting course, comprising different sections
on subjects such as time management, writing skills and communicating.
'The tutor's been fantastic, visiting me and discussing any problems – and
my boss has been very understanding too. If I'd had to go to college I would
always have had the worry of getting there on time and if I'd had to miss a
week I'd have found it difficult to catch up. This way I can work at home and
be flexible about my timing. It's a great confidence booster.'

9 The bottom line – help with funding

If you want to go for education and training to improve your skills levels, it may cost you money. Lack of finance can prove a tremendous barrier, but there are ways around the problem.

You may be eligible for a **grant** or **bursary** to help with course fees and additional costs such as transport, books, equipment and living expenses – whatever your age. Eligibility can be complex and depends on:

▌ the course you are applying for
▌ your individual circumstances
▌ the policy of your local education authority.

You need to contact your local education authority (LEA), which will be able to give you the latest details about grants, fees and other information relating to education and training costs.

If you are thinking of taking a **training course**, contact your local TEC or the Jobcentre. They may be able to help. If you have been unemployed or receiving benefit, you may be entitled to an allowance equal to benefit plus £10 a week. Fees for course tuition and books will be met and there may also be help with transport and childcare costs.

Find out whether an **employee development scheme** is a possibility at work – where your employer will pay some, if not all, of the costs of a course. (Read more about them on page 63.) If your employers have never heard of such schemes, they should get in touch with the local Training and Enterprise Council, or Local Enterprise Company in Scotland, and ask what help they can offer. TECs/LECs may also be able to help if you are aiming to work towards an **S/NVQ** – they are keen to encourage employers to train their workforce towards nationally recognised qualifications.

If you are considering a course at an **adult education centre, community centre** or **sixth form college**, you will find that there is usually a charge. But if you are unemployed or on a low income, you can often get special rates. At an **adult residential college**, all students on full-time courses receive a bursary which covers fees, residence and dependants' allowances. Ask colleges for further details.

Open learning courses (with the Open University, for example) all require a fee, but you may be allowed to pay in instalments. For some courses you may get help from your LEA or employer. If you are claiming benefit you could be eligible for reduced rates.

If you are opting for a **higher education** course at undergraduate level you may qualify for a **mandatory award** and a **student loan**. However, you should note that these arrangements differ for new students in 1998 from the arrangements for existing students. From 1998/99, if you are starting in full-time higher education and are eligible for a mandatory award, you (and your parents or spouse) will be asked to make a contribution towards fees of up to £1000 a year. You or your family may also be asked to make a contribution towards maintenance. About 30% of students (where parental income is taken into account) will make no contribution.

Support for living costs will be through grant and loan, but the maximum grant will be reduced and the loan increased, so that about three-quarters of the maximum support available comes from the loan and the rest from the grant. The grant will be means-tested as now, but the loan will not be. However, families will contribute no more to fees and maintenance than they do to maintenance alone at the moment. In 1999/2000, the grant will be phased out and the basic support available will be entirely through a loan.

Currently, students must be aged under 50 to be eligible for a loan, but the government is reviewing this. Loan repayment arrangements will be different for new students from 1998/99. You will only begin repaying when your income reaches £10,000 per annum. Above that level the size of repayments, and therefore the length of the repayment period, will depend directly on your income. Repayments will be made direct from your salary through the Inland Revenue. There will not be a fixed repayment period. The size of repayments will adjust with your income until the loan is repaid or cancelled. For example, if your income was £17,000pa you would pay back £52 a month. If your income was £20,000pa, you would pay back about £75 a month. Loans will be indexed to inflation, so that you will repay the same in real terms as you borrow.

Extra support is available for students who find themselves in particular difficulty or, for example, if they have children to support.

Students who are not eligible for a mandatory award have previously been able to apply for discretionary awards from local authorities. The government intends to introduce new arrangements for these students and is currently considering the best approach. The new arrangements will be designed to be more consistent across the country and more effective in helping students most in need. However, local authorities will be allowed to continue making discretionary payments to students if they wish to do so.

More information on support for higher education courses is in the booklet *Student Fees, Grants and Loans* (see page 82) and copies will be available from LEAs, universities, colleges and schools, or ring for a free copy on 0800 731 9133.

If you are intending to do a job-related course that lasts for up to two years but you can't afford to pay for it, you could apply for a **career development loan**. The loans are available through a partnership between the Department for Education and Employment and four major high street banks – Barclays, The Co-operative, Clydesdale, and The Royal Bank of Scotland. You can apply to borrow between £200 and £8000 to cover 80% of your course fees (sometimes 100%), as well as the full cost of books, materials and other expenses such as childcare. Repayments are deferred for the length of the course and up to a further month – or up to six months if you are unemployed when your repayments should start. Contact your local TEC for details or phone free on 0800 585505 between 9am and 9pm, Monday to Friday.

The European Social Fund (ESF) contributes towards the running costs of vocational training, guidance and counselling and employment support projects. Funding is available through a number of Objectives. Objectives 1, 2 and 5b cover specific designated regions and aim to regenerate areas which are currently underdeveloped or seriously affected by industrial or rural decline. Objective 3 is aimed at combating long-term unemployment. Individuals cannot apply for funding directly but any legally constituted organisation can – such as a local authority, college, voluntary organisation, TEC or LEC.

If you are not eligible for a grant, it is always worth finding out about grant-making trusts, to see whether you could get support from a charity. There should be a copy of the *Directory of Grant-Making Trusts* in your local library.

If you are a UK resident taking a **vocational** course leading to an NVQ, you may get basic **tax relief** on the fees for the course. If you are paying your own fees and not receiving assistance under any government schemes, you need pay only 75% of the course fees. If you are over 30, you may be able to claim for courses other than vocational courses. Ask your training provider for details, and read 'Tax relief for vocational training, Personal taxpayers Leaflet IR119', available from Inland Revenue offices.

You could be entitled to take advantage of the **21-hour rule** if you are:

∎ out of work
∎ have not been in full-time education for three months
∎ living on Income Support.

The 21-hour rule allows unemployed people to carry on claiming benefits while they are studying part time. Before you enrol on a course you need to check with the Benefits Agency to make sure that it won't affect your status as available for work or actively seeking employment. The Admissions Tutor at your college will be able to give you more information, and read *A Guide to Income Support*, issued by the Benefits Agency.

If you are hoping to fund a course in **Europe** you need to check with your college to see whether your local education authority can provide a grant. Tuition costs are not particularly high in the EU, so you may be able to afford to pay for a course yourself. But you will have to prove that you have sufficient means to support yourself and pay the fees.

If you are offered a place at the European University Institute in Florence, the Department for Education and Employment may give you a grant and pay some expenses. Contact the Postgraduate Awards Department (the address is on page 84). The Cultural Department of the Belgian Embassy in Eaton Square offers a number of postgraduate scholarships each year to the College of Europe in Bruges. The upper age limit is 30. Contact the UK Committee for the College of Europe (the address is on page 85).

Socrates is an EU programme that covers language training, open and distance learning and exchanges of information and experience as well as school and higher education (the address is on page 84).

In brief

Contact anyone who can give you information, for example:
- Local Education Authority
- Training and Enterprise Council or Local Enterprise Company in Scotland
- college
- Citizens' Advice Bureau.

You need the will to take control and the conviction to find the resources to invest in yourself – for a more employable future.

Where to find out more

Further reading

There are plenty of books that could be helpful if you are planning to develop your employment skills. Here are a few to be going on with. Some are free; some are not – check with the publisher; although your local library or careers office may have copies. The publishers addresses are listed at the end of this book section.

Adult Learners Week – free booklet available from NIACE.

Awards and Loans to Students: A Brief Guide (Northern Ireland). Available free from local Education and Library Boards or The Department of Education Student Support Branch, Ireland.

Build Your Own Rainbow – exercises designed to help you analyse and develop your personal skills, aptitudes and ambitions. It provides the key to a number of essential career development skills. Available from Trotman.

Courses Magazine. Comprehensive regional listing of courses published four times a year. Available from newsagents or from Tryfax.

Guide to Students' Allowances. Available free from The Student Awards Agency for Scotland.

Higher Education in the European Community. Available from bookshops or mail order from: HMSO (quote ISBN 92 826 0739 9).

How to Pass A-levels and GNVQs. Published by Kogan Page.

How to Pass Exams Without Anxiety. Available from Trotman.

How to Win as a Part-Time Student. Published by Kogan Page.

It's Your Chance – a national guide to adult education and training opportunities. A user-friendly and helpful paperback packed with useful ideas and encouragement. Published by COIC.

Make It Happen! – the Personal Action Learning PLAN. Published by Campaign for Learning.

Mature Students' Guide. Published by Trotman

Moving Ahead – Coming Back to Education. A handbook for adults. Published by Hobsons.

NVQs and How To Get Them. Published by Kogan Page.

Register of Recognised Access Courses to Higher Education. A comprehensive register giving brief details of kitemarked (indicating approval by the British Standards Institution) Access courses throughout the UK. Available in libraries and guidance centres and from ECCTIS 2000.

Returning to Work: A Guide for Lone Parents. Published by the National Council for One Parent Families.

Second Chances – the guide to adult education and training opportunities. A comprehensive directory of options and opportunities throughout the UK. Published by COIC.

Setting up in Business: A Guide To Regulatory Requirements and *Make the Cash Flow*. Available free from DTI Publications.

Skills Focus series: *Boosting Your Career Prospects; Creating Winning CVs and Applications; Exploring Career Opportunities; Promoting Yourself at Interview*. Published by Trotman.

Student Fees, Grants and Loans: A Brief Guide. Available from schools, colleges and LEA careers libraries or free from DfEE Publications.

Studying in Europe. Published by Hobsons Publishing.

Time to Learn – a directory of residential weekend and learning holidays. Published twice yearly, costing £4.95 (including p&p), available from bookshops or from NIACE.

Unemployment and Training Rights Handbook by Dann Finn. Published by the Unemployment Unit.

University and College Entrance and *Stepping Up*. Available free from: Universities and Colleges Admission Service (UCAS).

Working for Yourself: The Daily Telegraph Guide. Published by Kogan Page.

Working Parent's Handbook. Published by Parents At Work.

Publisher addresses

Campaign for Learning, RSA, 8 John Adam Street, London WC2N 6EZ. Tel: 0171 930 5115

Choice and Careers Division (previously COIC), Moorfoot, Sheffield S1 4PQ. Tel: 0114 259 3368

DfEE Publications Despatch Centre, PO Box 5000, Sudbury, Suffolk CO10 6YJ. Tel: 0850 602 2260

The Department of Education Student Support Branch, Rathgael House, Balloo Road, Bangor, County Down BT19 7PR. Tel: 01247 279279

DTI Publications, Admail 528, London SW1W 8YT

ECCTIS 2000, Oriel House, Oriel Road, Cheltenham, Gloucestershire GL50 1XP. Tel: 01242 252627

Hobsons Publishing, Bateman Street, Cambridge CB2 1LZ. Tel: 01223 354551

Kogan Page, 120 Pentonville Road, London N1 9BR. Tel: 0171 278 0433

National Council for One Parent Families, 255 Kentish Town Road, London NW5 2LX. Tel: 0171 267 1361

NIACE, 21 De Montfort Street, Leicester LE1 7GE. Tel: 0116 255 1451

Parents At Work, 45 Beech Street, London EC2Y 8AD. Tel: 0171 628 3578

The Student Awards Agency for Scotland, Gyleview House, 3 Redheughs Rigg, South Gyle, Edinburgh EH12 9HH. Tel: 0131 244 5823

Trotman & Company Ltd, 12 Hill Rise, Richmond, Surrey TW10 6UA. Tel: 0181 940 5668

Universities and Colleges Admission Service (UCAS), Fulton House, Jessop Avenue, Cheltenham, Gloucester GL50 3SH. Tel: 01242 222444

Unemployment Unit, 322 St John Street. London EC1V 4NT. Tel: 0171 833 1222

Useful addresses

The following might be useful in your quest for skills development.

Basic skills

For information about improving skills such as literacy and numeracy, including the name of a local contact:
Basic Skills Agency, Commonwealth House, 1–19 New Oxford Street, London WC1A 1NU. Tel: 0171 405 4017. Phone free on 0800 700 987 to be put through to one of 350 recognised national referral points.

Women returners

Women Returners Network, 100 Park Village East, London NW1 3SR. Tel: 0171 468 2290. Works with industry, commerce, training and educational organisations to make it easier for women to re-enter education, training and employment.

New Ways to Work, 309 Upper Street, London N1 2TY. Tel: 0171 226 4026. Helps individuals, employers and organisations develop flexible working arrangements.

Childcare

Working for Childcare, 77 Holloway Road, London N7 8JZ. Tel: 0171 700 0281/2. Promotes the development of quality childcare to meet the needs of working parents and their children. Can give advice on setting up nurseries.

Parents at Work, 5th Floor, 45 Beech Street, Barbican, London EC2P 2LZ. Advice line: 0171 628 3578

National Council for One Parent Families, 255 Kentish Town Road, London NW5 2LX. Tel: 0171 267 1361

People with disabilities

SKILL: National Bureau for Students with Disabilities, 336 Brixton Road, London SW9 7AA. Tel: 0171 274 7840

Mencap Employment Service, National Centre, 123 Golden Lane, London EC1Y 0RT. Tel: 0171 454 0454

Open learning

The Open Learning Directory, published annually by Pergamon Press, provides comprehensive information about packages of learning materials. It is available in your local careers library.

National Extension College (NEC), 18 Brooklands Avenue, Cambridge CB2 2HN. Tel: 01223 316644

Financial Times Management, Portland Tower, Portland Street, Manchester M1 3LD. Tel: 0161 245 3300

Open College of the Arts. Houndhill, Worsborough, Barnsley, South Yorkshire, S70 6TU. Information line: 0891 168902

Open University, Central Enquiries, PO Box 200, Milton Keynes MK7 6AA. Tel: 01908 653231. Course Reservation Centre, Milton Keynes MK7 6ZS

Adult Education Residential Colleges Association (ARCA), Wansfell College, 30 Piercing Hill, Theydon Bois, Essex CM16 7LF. Tel: 01992 813027

Learning in Europe

European Commission. 8 Storey's Gate, London SW1P 3AT. Tel: 0171 973 1992

Central Bureau for Educational Visits and Exchanges, 10 Spring Gardens, London SW1A 2BN. Tel: 0171 389 4004

SOCRATES Programme, Department for Education and Employment, Caxton House, Tothill Street, London SW1 9NF. Tel: 0171 273 3000

Postgraduate Awards Department. Department for Education and Employment (DfEE), Room 214, Mowden Hall, Staindrop Road, Darlington DL3 9BG. Tel: 01325 460155

UK Committee for the College of Europe. UACES Secretariat, King's College, Strand, London WC2R 2LS. Tel: 0171 873 2377

Funding

Career Development Loans. Run by the Department for Education and Employment in conjunction with four high street banks. Phone free on 0800 585505 Monday to Friday, 9am–9pm

The Department of Social Security may pay benefits to certain students. Contact your local Benefits Agency office or ring the free telephone enquiry service: Social Security 0800 666555; Urdu: 0800 289188; Punjabi: 0800 521360; Chinese: 0800 25245; Welsh: 0800 289011

Self-employment

Business in the Community (England), 44 Baker Street, London W1M 1DH. Tel: 0171 224 1600

Business in the Community (Ireland), BP Oil UK Ltd, Airport Road West, Belfast BT3 9EA. Tel: 01232 739639

Scottish Business in the Community, 30 Hanover Street, Edinburgh EH2 2DR. Tel: 0131 220 3001

LEDU, Upper Galwally, Belfast, Northern Ireland BT8 6TB. Tel: 01232 491031

Other useful organisations

Workers Education Association (WEA), National Office, Temple House, 17 Victoria Park Square, London E2 9PB. Tel: 0181 983 151. A voluntary body providing education and training for adults.

NIACE – National Institute of Adult Continuing Education, 21 de Montfort Street, Leicester LE1 7GE. Tel: 0116 2551 451

Careers information specialists

Career Options for Adults provides a range of services for individuals looking for careers advice. Services include CV and jobsearch and preparing for an assessment centre. Some services are free to unemployed clients.
Contact: Linda Smith,
193–196 Chelmer Gate,
Chelmsford, Essex CM2 0LG
Tel: 01245 706870
Fax: 01245 706850

Careers Enterprise Group is one of the leading careers service companies in the country, providing the careers services in Buckinghamshire and Milton Keynes, Kent, Surrey and Hackney, Islington and the City of London.
Contact: Heather Darlington, Sutton House, Weyside Park, Catteshall Lane, Godalming, Surrey GU7 1XJ
Tel: 01483 413200
Fax: 01483 413201
E-mail: info@surreycareers.co.uk

Progressions Ltd is a new software house which combines expertise in developing databases with careers information and guidance. Since April 1998, Progressions has also been responsible for the sale and development of JIIG CAL software products.
Contact: Amanda King, Sutton House, Weyside Park, Catteshall Lane, Godalming, Surrey GU7 1XJ
Tel: 01483 413200
Fax: 01483 413201
E-mail: info@progressions. co.uk
Web site: http://www.progressions.co.uk

Further education and specialist colleges

Beckenham Secretarial & Business College offers a wide variety of Secretarial, Computer and Shorthand courses and specialises in providing a high standard of tutor led training at all levels. Small classes, friendly atmosphere, flexible hours.
Contact: Elizabeth Wakeling,
31 Beckenham Road, Beckenham, Kent BR3 4PR
Tel: 0181 650 3321
Fax: 0181 650 3321

Dean College of London offers a range of courses in GCSE, A-level, University Access, Business Administration, Computing and Secretarial, Preparation for Employment and Degree Studies. Dean College is BAC Accredited.
Contact: Dr A Andreou,
97/101 Seven Sisters Road,
Holloway, London N7 7QP
Tel: 0171 281 4461
Fax: 0171 281 7849

Lord Mayor Treloar College.
The Lord Mayor Treloar National Specialist College provides residential care, education, therapy and medical support for young people with physical and learning disabilities. Courses include NVQs/GNVQs, A-levels and ASDAN Awards.
Contact: Helen Burton,
Admissions Officer, Holybourne, Alton, Hants GU34 4EN
Tel: 01420 547425
E-mail: admissions@treloar.org.uk

St James College. London's premier business training college. 1, 2, and 3 term courses, incorporating Typing, IT, Shorthand and Business Skills. Flexibility, quality and commitment ensure we can provide you with a head start.
Contact: Andrew Williams,
4 Wetherby Gardens,
London SW5 0JN
Tel: 0171 373 3852
Fax: 0171 370 3303

University of Wales Aberystwyth offers a wide range of courses in arts and humanities, business and finance, biological sciences and biotechnology, equine and agricultural science, geography and physical sciences, law and film studies.
Contact: Dr Russel Davies, Old College, King Street, Aberystwyth SY23 2AX. Tel: 01970 623111
Fax: 01970 627410
E-mail: undergraduate-admissions @aber.ac.uk.
Web site:www.aber.ac.uk

Institutions/industry training organisations

Chartered Institute of Management Accountants. The professional and examining body for Chartered Management Accountants. CIMA is considered by employers worldwide the most relevant financial qualification for business today.
Contact: Registry, 63 Portland Place, London W1N 4AB.
Tel: 0171 9179251.
Fax: 0171 2551462
E-mail: mw-registry@cima.org.uk
Web site: www.cima.org.uk

National Training Organisation for Information Technology
The ITNTO sets standards for a world class IT community, spearheads the UK's development of IT skills and influences the provision of IT education and training.
Contact: Anne Russell, 16 Berners Street, London, W1P 3DD
Tel: 0171 580 6677.
Fax: 0171 580 5577.
E-mail: info@into.org.uk.
Web site: http://www.into.org.uk

Language schools

EF International Language Schools provides intensive language courses for adults of 16 years and over. Students learn on location, studying in an international environment while living among native speakers to maximise exposure to the language and culture.
Contact: Ian McKenzie, Kensington Cloisters, 5 Kensington Church Street, London W8 4LD
Tel: 0171 878 3550
Fax: 0171 795 6625
E-mail: gbs.london @ef.com.
Web site: www.ef.com

Language Studies International offers evening courses, 1:1 tuition and in-company training in English and over 30 foreign languages in London and at centres around the world.
Contact: Sarah McKechnie,
19–21 Ridgmount Street,
London W4E 7AH
Tel: 0171 467 6500. Fax: 0171 323 1736. E-mail: lon@lsi.edu
Web site: http://www.lsi.edu

Opportunities overseas: employment

Council on International Educational Exchange is a non-profit organisation which offers work abroad programmes to the USA, Australia, China, Japan and Canada, as well as study abroad programmes to 23 countries worldwide.
Contact: David Preston,
52 Poland Street, London W1V 4JQ
Tel: 0171 478 2000
Fax: 0171 734 7322
E-mail: infouk@ciee.org
Web site: www.ciee.org

Opportunities overseas: study

Language Studies International offers evening courses, 1:1 tuition and in-company training in English and over 30 foreign languages in London and at centres around the world.
Contact: Sarah McKechnie,
19–21 Ridgmount Street London,
W4E 7AH
Tel: 0171 467 6500
Fax: 0171 323 1736
E-mail: lon@lsi.edu
Web site: http://www.lsi.edu.

Training providers

Council for Awards in Children's Care and Education. CACHE specialises in training and assessment for Early Years Care and Education, and Playwork. It is an awarding body for NVQs, initial training courses and professional development awards for anyone working with young children, or in playwork.
Contact: Alex Bellamy,
8 Chequer Street, St Albans,
Herts AL1 3XZ
Tel: 01727 847636
Fax: 01727 867609
E-mail: CACHE@compuserve.com
Web site: http://ourworld.compu-serve.com/homepages/CACHE

Typehouse Training offers intensive 'quick skills' courses 3–12 weeks or individual subjects. Office 97, Word, Excel, Powerpoint, Access, Accounts, Shorthand, Touch Typing, DTP. Start every monday.
Contact: Sarah Montague,
3A Harrington Road, South Kensington, London SW7 3ES
Tel: 0171 823 9991
Fax: 0171 584 6890